Ephesians
Philippians
Colossians
Philemon

D1611442

ABOUT THE AUTHORS

General Editor; Ephesians; Colossians:

Clinton E. Arnold (PhD, University of Aberdeen), professor and chairman, department of New Testament, Talbot School of Theology, Biola University, Los Angeles, California

Philippians:

Frank Thielman (PhD, Duke University), Presbyterian professor of divinity, Beeson Divinity School, Samford University, Birmingham, Alabama

Philemon:

S. M. Baugh (PhD, University of California, Irvine), associate professor of New Testament, Westminster Theological Seminary in California, Escondido, California

Zondervan Illustrated Bible Backgrounds Commentary

Ephesians
Philippians
Colossians
Philemon

Clinton E. Arnold
Frank S. Thielman
S. M. Baugh

Clinton E. Arnold   *general editor*

ZONDERVAN®

ZONDERVAN.com/
AUTHORTRACKER
follow your favorite authors

ZONDERVAN®

Zondervan Illustrated Bible Backgrounds Commentary:
    Ephesians and Colossians—Copyright © 2002 by Clinton E. Arnold
    Philippians—Copyright © 2002 by Frank S. Thielman
    Philemon—Copyright © 2002 by Steven M. Baugh

Requests for information should be addressed to:

Zondervan, *Grand Rapids, Michigan 49530*

Library of Congress Cataloging-in-Publication Data
    Zondervan illustrated Bible backgrounds commentary / Clinton E. Arnold, general editor.
        p.cm.
    Includes bibliographical references.
    ISBN-10: 0-310-27827-9
    ISBN-13: 978-0-310-27827-6
    1. Bible. N.T.—Commentaries.   I. Arnold, Clinton E.
    BS2341.52.Z66 2001
    225.7—dc21   2001046801
                                                                       CIP

Printed in China

Interior design by Sherri L. Hoffman

---

07 08 09 10 11 12 13 • 12 11 10 9 8 7 6 5 4 3 2 1

CONTENTS

INTRODUCTION

All readers of the Bible have a tendency to view what it says it through their own culture and life circumstances. This can happen almost subconsiously as we read the pages of the text.

When most people in the church read about the thief on the cross, for instance, they immediately think of a burglar that held up a store or broke into a home. They may be rather shocked to find out that the guy was actually a Jewish revolutionary figure who was part of a growing movement in Palestine eager to throw off Roman rule.

It also comes as something of a surprise to contemporary Christians that "cursing" in the New Testament era had little or nothing to do with cussing somebody out. It had far more to do with the invocation of spirits to cause someone harm.

No doubt there is a need in the church for learning more about the world of the New Testament to avoid erroneous interpretations of the text of Scripture. But relevant historical and cultural insights also provide an added dimension of perspective to the words of the Bible. This kind of information often functions in the same way as watching a movie in color rather than in black and white. Finding out, for instance, how Paul compared Christ's victory on the cross to a joyous celebration parade in honor of a Roman general after winning an extraordinary battle brings does indeed magnify the profundity and implications of Jesus' work on the cross. Discovering that the factions at Corinth ("I follow Paul . . . I follow Apollos . . .") had plenty of precedent in the local cults ("I follow Aphrodite; I follow Apollo . . .") helps us understand the "why" of a particular problem. Learning about the water supply from the springs of Hierapolis that flowed into Laodicea as "lukewarm" water enables us to appreciate the relevance of the metaphor Jesus used when he addressed the spiritual laxity of this church.

My sense is that most Christians are eager to learn more about the real life setting of the New Testament. In the preaching and teaching of the Bible in the church, congregants are always grateful when they learn something of the background and historical context of the text. It not only helps them understand the text more accurately, but often enables them to identify with the people and circumstances of the Bible. I have been asked on countless occasions by Christians, "Where can I get access to good historical background information about this passage?" Earnest Christians are hungry for information that makes their Bibles come alive.

The stimulus for this commentary came from the church and the aim is to serve the church. The contributors to this series have sought to provide illuminating and interesting historical/cultural background information. The intent was to draw upon relevant papyri, inscriptions, archaeological discoveries, and the numerous studies of Judaism, Roman culture, Hellenism, and other features of the world of the New Testament and to make the results accessible to people in the church. We recognize that some readers of the commentary will want to go further, and so the sources of the information have been carefully documented in endnotes.

The written information has been supplemented with hundreds of photographs, maps, charts, artwork, and other graphics that help the reader better understand the world of the New Testament. Each of the writers was given an opportunity to dream up a "wish list" of illustrations that he thought would help to illustrate the passages in the New Testament book for which he was writing commentary. Although we were not able to obtain everything they were looking for, we came close.

The team of commentators are writing for the benefit of the broad array of Christians who simply want to better understand their Bibles from the vantage point of the historical context. This is an installment in a new genre of "Bible background" commentaries that was kicked off by Craig Keener's fine volume. Consequently, this is not an "exegetical" commentary that provides linguistic insight and background into Greek constructions and verb tenses. Neither is this work an "expository" commentary that provides a verse-by-verse exposition of the text; for in-depth philological or theological insight, readers will need to have other more specialized or comprehensive commentaries available. Nor is this an "historical-critical" commentary, although the contributors are all scholars and have already made substantial academic contributions on the New Testament books they are writing on for this set. The team intentionally does not engage all of the issues that are discussed in the scholarly guild.

Rather, our goal is to offer a reading and interpretation of the text informed by what we regard as the most relevant historical information. For many in the church, this commentary will serve as an important entry point into the interpretation and appreciation of the text. For other more serious students of the Word, these volumes will provide an important supplement to many of the fine exegetical, expository, and critical available.

The contributors represent a group of scholars who embrace the Bible as the Word of God and believe that the message of its pages has life-changing relevance for faith and practice today. Accordingly, we offer "Reflections" on the relevance of the Scripture to life for every chapter of the New Testament.

I pray that this commentary brings you both delight and insight in digging deeper into the Word of God.

Clinton E. Arnold
General Editor

LIST OF SIDEBARS

LIST OF CHARTS

INDEX OF PHOTOS AND MAPS

ABBREVIATIONS

1. Books of the Bible and Apocrypha

1 Chron.	1 Chronicles
2 Chron.	2 Chronicles
1 Cor.	1 Corinthians
2 Cor.	2 Corinthians
1 Esd.	1 Esdras
2 Esd.	2 Esdras
1 John	1 John
2 John	2 John
3 John	3 John
1 Kings	1 Kings
2 Kings	2 Kings
1 Macc.	1 Maccabees
2 Macc.	2 Maccabees
1 Peter	1 Peter
2 Peter	2 Peter
1 Sam.	1 Samuel
2 Sam.	2 Samuel
1 Thess.	1 Thessalonians
2 Thess.	2 Thessalonians
1 Tim.	1 Timothy
2 Tim.	2 Timothy
Acts	Acts
Amos	Amos
Bar.	Baruch
Bel	Bel and the Dragon
Col.	Colossians
Dan.	Daniel
Deut.	Deuteronomy
Eccl.	Ecclesiastes
Ep. Jer.	Epistle of Jeremiah
Eph.	Ephesians
Est.	Esther
Ezek.	Ezekiel
Ex.	Exodus
Ezra	Ezra
Gal.	Galatians
Gen.	Genesis
Hab.	Habakkuk
Hag.	Haggai
Heb.	Hebrews
Hos.	Hosea
Isa.	Isaiah
James	James
Jer.	Jeremiah
Job	Job
Joel	Joel
John	John
Jonah	Jonah
Josh.	Joshua
Jude	Jude
Judg.	Judges
Judith	Judith
Lam.	Lamentations
Lev.	Leviticus
Luke	Luke
Mal.	Malachi
Mark	Mark
Matt.	Matthew
Mic.	Micah
Nah.	Nahum
Neh.	Nehemiah
Num.	Numbers
Obad.	Obadiah
Phil.	Philippians
Philem.	Philemon
Pr. Man.	Prayer of Manassah
Prov.	Proverbs
Ps.	Psalm
Rest. of Est.	The Rest of Esther
Rev.	Revelation
Rom.	Romans
Ruth	Ruth
S. of III Ch.	The Song of the Three Holy Children
Sir.	Sirach/Ecclesiasticus
Song	Song of Songs
Sus.	Susanna
Titus	Titus
Tobit	Tobit
Wisd. Sol.	The Wisdom of Solomon
Zech.	Zechariah
Zeph.	Zephaniah

2. Old and New Testament Pseudepigrapha and Rabbinic Literature

Individual tractates of rabbinic literature follow the abbreviations of the *SBL Handbook of Style*, pp. 79–80. Qumran documents follow standard Dead Sea Scroll conventions.

2 Bar.	*2 Baruch*
3 Bar.	*3 Baruch*
4 Bar.	*4 Baruch*
1 En.	*1 Enoch*
2 En.	*2 Enoch*
3 En.	*3 Enoch*
4 Ezra	*4 Ezra*

3 Macc.	3 Maccabees
4 Macc.	4 Maccabees
5 Macc.	5 Maccabees
Acts Phil.	Acts of Philip
Acts Pet.	Acts of Peter and the 12 Apostles
Apoc. Elijah	Apocalypse of Elijah
As. Mos.	Assumption of Moses
b.	Babylonian Talmud (+ tractate)
Gos. Thom.	Gospel of Thomas
Jos. Asen.	Joseph and Aseneth
Jub.	Jubilees
Let. Aris.	Letter of Aristeas
m.	Mishnah (+ tractate)
Mek.	Mekilta
Midr.	Midrash I (+ biblical book)
Odes Sol.	Odes of Solomon
Pesiq. Rab.	Pesiqta Rabbati
Pirqe. R. El.	Pirqe Rabbi Eliezer
Pss. Sol.	Psalms of Solomon
Rab.	Rabbah (+biblical book); (e.g., Gen. Rab.=Genesis Rabbah)
S. ʿOlam Rab.	Seder ʿOlam Rabbah
Sem.	Semahot
Sib. Or.	Sibylline Oracles
T. Ab.	Testament of Abraham
T. Adam	Testament of Adam
T. Ash.	Testament of Asher
T. Benj.	Testament of Benjamin
T. Dan	Testament of Dan
T. Gad	Testament of Gad
T. Hez.	Testament of Hezekiah
T. Isaac	Testament of Isaac
T. Iss.	Testament of Issachar
T. Jac.	Testament of Jacob
T. Job	Testament of Job
T. Jos.	Testament of Joseph
T. Jud.	Testament of Judah
T. Levi	Testament of Levi
T. Mos.	Testament of Moses
T. Naph.	Testament of Naphtali
T. Reu.	Testament of Reuben
T. Sim.	Testament of Simeon
T. Sol.	Testament of Solomon
T. Zeb.	Testament of Zebulum
Tanh.	Tanhuma
Tg. Isa.	Targum of Isaiah
Tg. Lam.	Targum of Lamentations
Tg. Neof.	Targum Neofiti
Tg. Onq.	Targum Onqelos
Tg. Ps.-J	Targum Pseudo-Jonathan
y.	Jerusalem Talmud (+ tractate)

3. Classical Historians

For an extended list of classical historians and church fathers, see *SBL Handbook of Style*, pp. 84–

87. For many works of classical antiquity, the abbreviations have been subjected to the author's discretion; the names of these works should be obvious upon consulting entries of the classical writers in classical dictionaries or encyclopedias.

Eusebius

Eccl. Hist.	Ecclesiastical History

Josephus

Ag. Ap.	Against Apion
Ant.	Jewish Antiquities
J.W.	Jewish War
Life	The Life

Philo

Abraham	On the Life of Abraham
Agriculture	On Agriculture
Alleg. Interp	Allegorical Interpretation
Animals	Whether Animals Have Reason
Cherubim	On the Cherubim
Confusion	On the Confusion of Thomas
Contempl. Life	On the Contemplative Life
Creation	On the Creation of the World
Curses	On Curses
Decalogue	On the Decalogue
Dreams	On Dreams
Drunkenness	On Drunkenness
Embassy	On the Embassy to Gaius
Eternity	On the Eternity of the World
Flaccus	Against Flaccus
Flight	On Flight and Finding
Giants	On Giants
God	On God
Heir	Who Is the Heir?
Hypothetica	Hypothetica
Joseph	On the Life of Joseph
Migration	On the Migration of Abraham
Moses	On the Life of Moses
Names	On the Change of Names
Person	That Every Good Person Is Free
Planting	On Planting
Posterity	On the Posterity of Cain
Prelim. Studies	On the Preliminary Studies
Providence	On Providence
QE	Questions and Answers on Exodus
QG	Questions and Answers on Genesis
Rewards	On Rewards and Punishments
Sacrifices	On the Sacrifices of Cain and Abel
Sobriety	On Sobriety
Spec. Laws	On the Special Laws
Unchangeable	That God Is Unchangeable
Virtues	On the Virtues

Worse	*That the Worse Attacks the Better*

Apostolic Fathers

1 Clem.	*First Letter of Clement*
Barn.	*Epistle of Barnabas*
Clem. Hom.	*Ancient Homily of Clement* (also called *2 Clement*)
Did.	*Didache*
Herm. Vis.; Sim.	*Shepherd of Hermas, Visions; Similitudes*
Ignatius	*Epistles of Ignatius* (followed by the letter's name)
Mart. Pol.	*Martyrdom of Polycarp*

4. Modern Abbreviations

AASOR	Annual of the American Schools of Oriental Research
AB	Anchor Bible
ABD	*Anchor Bible Dictionary*
ABRL	Anchor Bible Reference Library
AGJU	Arbeiten zur Geschichte des antiken Judentums und des Urchristentums
AH	*Agricultural History*
ALGHJ	Arbeiten zur Literatur und Geschichte des Hellenistischen Judentums
AnBib	Analecta biblica
ANRW	*Aufstieg und Niedergang der römischen Welt*
ANTC	Abingdon New Testament Commentaries
BAGD	Bauer, W., W. F. Arndt, F. W. Gingrich, and F. W. Danker. *Greek-English Lexicon of the New Testament and Other Early Christina Literature* (2d. ed.)
BA	*Biblical Archaeologist*
BAFCS	Book of Acts in Its First Century Setting
BAR	*Biblical Archaeology Review*
BASOR	*Bulletin of the American Schools of Oriental Research*
BBC	*Bible Background Commentary*
BBR	*Bulletin for Biblical Research*
BDB	Brown, F., S. R. Driver, and C. A. Briggs. *A Hebrew and English Lexicon of the Old Testament*
BDF	Blass, F., A. Debrunner, and R. W. Funk. *A Greek Grammar of the New Testament and Other Early Christian Literature*
BECNT	Baker Exegetical Commentary on the New Testament
BI	*Biblical Illustrator*
Bib	*Biblica*
BibSac	*Bibliotheca Sacra*

BLT	Brethren Life and Thought
BNTC	Black's New Testament Commentary
BRev	*Bible Review*
BSHJ	Baltimore Studies in the History of Judaism
BST	The Bible Speaks Today
BSV	Biblical Social Values
BT	*The Bible Translator*
BTB	Biblical Theology Bulletin
BZ	Biblische Zeitschrift
CBQ	Catholic Biblical Quarterly
CBTJ	Calvary Baptist Theological Journal
CGTC	Cambridge Greek Testament Commentary
CH	*Church History*
CIL	*Corpus inscriptionum latinarum*
CPJ	*Corpus papyrorum judaicorum*
CRINT	*Compendia rerum iudaicarum ad Novum Testamentum*
CTJ	*Calvin Theological Journal*
CTM	*Concordia Theological Monthly*
CTT	Contours of Christian Theology
DBI	*Dictionary of Biblical Imagery*
DCM	*Dictionary of Classical Mythology.*
DDD	*Dictionary of Deities and Demons in the Bible*
DJBP	*Dictionary of Judaism in the Biblical Period*
DJG	*Dictionary of Jesus and the Gospels*
DLNT	*Dictionary of the Later New Testament and Its Developments*
DNTB	*Dictionary of New Testament Background*
DPL	*Dictionary of Paul and His Letters*
EBC	*Expositor's Bible Commentary*
EDBT	*Evangelical Dictionary of Biblical Theology*
EDNT	*Exegetical Dictionary of the New Testament*
EJR	*Encyclopedia of the Jewish Religion*
EPRO	Études préliminaires aux religions orientales dans l'empire romain
EvQ	*Evangelical Quarterly*
ExpTim	*Expository Times*
FRLANT	Forschungen zur Religion und Literatur des Alten und Neuen Testament
GNC	Good News Commentary
GNS	Good News Studies
HCNT	*Hellenistic Commentary to the New Testament*
HDB	*Hastings Dictionary of the Bible*

HJP	History of the Jewish People in the Age of Jesus Christ, by E. Schürer	NEAE	New Encyclopedia of Archaeological Excavations in the Holy Land
HTR	Harvard Theological Review		
HTS	Harvard Theological Studies	NEASB	Near East Archaeological Society Bulletin
HUCA	Hebrew Union College Annual		
IBD	Illustrated Bible Dictionary	New Docs	New Documents Illustrating Early Christianity
IBS	Irish Biblical Studies		
ICC	International Critical Commentary	NIBC	New International Biblical Commentary
IDB	The Interpreter's Dictionary of the Bible	NICNT	New International Commentary on the New Testament
IEJ	Israel Exploration Journal	NIDNTT	New International Dictionary of New Testament Theology
IG	Inscriptiones graecae		
IGRR	Inscriptiones graecae ad res romanas pertinentes	NIGTC	New International Greek Testament Commentary
ILS	Inscriptiones Latinae Selectae	NIVAC	NIV Application Commentary
Imm	Immanuel	NorTT	Norsk Teologisk Tidsskrift
ISBE	International Standard Bible Encyclopedia	NoT	Notes on Translation
		NovT	Novum Testamentum
Int	Interpretation	NovTSup	Novum Testamentum Supplements
IvE	Inschriften von Ephesos		
IVPNTC	InterVarsity Press New Testament Commentary	NTAbh	Neutestamentliche Abhandlungen
JAC	Jahrbuch fur Antike und Christentum	NTS	New Testament Studies
		NTT	New Testament Theology
JBL	Journal of Biblical Literature	NTTS	New Testament Tools and Studies
JETS	Journal of the Evangelical Theological Society		
		OAG	Oxford Archaeological Guides
JHS	Journal of Hellenic Studies	OCCC	Oxford Companion to Classical Civilization
JJS	Journal of Jewish Studies		
JOAIW	Jahreshefte des Osterreeichischen Archaologischen Instites in Wien	OCD	Oxford Classical Dictionary
		ODCC	The Oxford Dictionary of the Christian Church
JSJ	Journal for the Study of Judaism in the Persian, Hellenistic, and Roman Periods	OGIS	Orientis graeci inscriptiones selectae
		OHCW	The Oxford History of the Classical World
JRS	Journal of Roman Studies		
JSNT	Journal for the Study of the New Testament	OHRW	Oxford History of the Roman World
JSNTSup	Journal for the Study of the New Testament: Supplement Series	OTP	Old Testament Pseudepigrapha, ed. by J. H. Charlesworth
JSOT	Journal for the Study of the Old Testament		
		PEQ	Palestine Exploration Quarterly
JSOTSup	Journal for the Study of the Old Testament: Supplement Series	PG	Patrologia graeca
		PGM	Papyri graecae magicae: Die griechischen Zauberpapyri
JTS	Journal of Theological Studies		
KTR	Kings Theological Review	PL	Patrologia latina
LCL	Loeb Classical Library	PNTC	Pelican New Testament Commentaries
LEC	Library of Early Christianity		
LSJ	Liddell, H. G., R. Scott, H. S. Jones. A Greek-English Lexicon	Rb	Revista biblica
		RB	Revue biblique
MM	Moulton, J. H., and G. Milligan. The Vocabulary of the Greek Testament	RivB	Rivista biblica italiana
		RTR	Reformed Theological Review
		SB	Sources bibliques
MNTC	Moffatt New Testament Commentary	SBL	Society of Biblical Literature
		SBLDS	Society of Biblical Literature Dissertation Series
NBD	New Bible Dictionary		
NC	Narrative Commentaries	SBLMS	Society of Biblical Literature Monograph Series
NCBC	New Century Bible Commentary Eerdmans		

SBLSP	*Society of Biblical Literature Seminar Papers*
SBS	Stuttgarter Bibelstudien
SBT	Studies in Biblical Theology
SCJ	*Stone-Campbell Journal*
Scr	*Scripture*
SE	*Studia Evangelica*
SEG	*Supplementum epigraphicum graecum*
SJLA	Studies in Judaism in Late Antiquity
SJT	*Scottish Journal of Theology*
SNTSMS	Society for New Testament Studies Monograph Series
SSC	Social Science Commentary
SSCSSG	Social-Science Commentary on the Synoptic Gospels
Str-B	Strack, H. L., and P. Billerbeck. *Kommentar zum Neuen Testament aus Talmud und Midrasch*
TC	Thornapple Commentaries
TDNT	*Theological Dictionary of the New Testament*
TDOT	*Theological Dictionary of the Old Testament*
TLNT	*Theological Lexicon of the New Testament*
TLZ	*Theologische Literaturzeitung*
TNTC	Tyndale New Testament Commentary
TrinJ	*Trinity Journal*
TS	*Theological Studies*
TSAJ	Texte und Studien zum antiken Judentum
TWNT	*Theologische Wörterbuch zum Neuen Testament*
TynBul	*Tyndale Bulletin*
WBC	Word Biblical Commentary Waco: Word, 1982
WMANT	Wissenschaftliche Monographien zum Alten und Neuen Testament
WUNT	Wissenschaftliche Untersuchungen zum Neuen Testament
YJS	Yale Judaica Series
ZNW	*Zeitschrift fur die neutestamentliche Wissenschaft und die Junde der alteren Kirche*
ZPE	*Zeischrift der Papyrolgie und Epigraphkik*
ZPEB	*Zondervan Pictorial Encyclopedia of the Bible*

5. General Abbreviations

ad. loc.	in the place cited
b.	born
c., ca.	circa
cf.	compare
d.	died
ed(s).	editors(s), edited by
e.g.	for example
ET	English translation
frg.	fragment
i.e.	that is
ibid.	in the same place
idem	the same (author)
lit.	literally
l(l)	line(s)
MSS	manuscripts
n.d.	no date
NS	New Series
par.	parallel
passim	here and there
repr.	reprint
ser.	series
s.v.	*sub verbo*, under the word
trans.	translator, translated by; transitive

Zondervan Illustrated Bible Backgrounds Commentary

EPHESIANS

by Clinton E. Arnold

Ephesus and Western Asia Minor

The city of Ephesus was the leading city of the richest region of the Roman empire. With a population of about 250,000 people, only Rome and Alexandria were larger. Ephesus served as the Roman provincial capital of Asia Minor and was a prosperous commercial center. As the principal port for Asia Minor, merchant and cargo vessels from all over the Mediterranean docked there to unload passengers and goods as well as to transport products from Asia Minor to Rome and throughout the empire. The first-century writer Strabo called Ephesus "the greatest commercial center in Asia this side of the Taurus river."[1]

The city was cosmopolitan and multiethnic. In addition to the indigenous Anatolian peoples of Ionia, Lydia, Phrygia, Caria, and Mysia, Ephesus was home to Egyptian, Greek, and Roman settlers. There was also a strong Jewish community in the city since Seleucid times (3d century B.C.). It appears that the Jews of the city had a fairly cordial relationship with the civic

EPHESUS

The countryside around the city.

> ## Ephesians
> ## IMPORTANT FACTS:
>
> - **AUTHOR:** The apostle Paul.
> - **DATE:** A.D. 60–61 (Paul imprisoned in Rome).
> - **OCCASION:**
>   - To give new believers converted from a background in Judaism, local religions, magic, and astrology a positive grounding in the gospel of Christ.
>   - To help and admonish believers to cultivate a distinctively Christian lifestyle.
> - **KEY THEMES:**
>   1. Christ is supreme over all of creation, especially the powers of darkness.
>   2. Believers participate with Christ in his death, resurrection, and fullness.
>   3. The church is the one body of Christ and is composed of Jews and Gentiles.

officials and the local populace since there is no evidence of the kind of ethnic strife that rocked Alexandria and Rome. According to Josephus, they had been granted freedom to practice their religion according to their own traditions.[2]

The Introduction of Christianity to the City

Paul started the church at Ephesus after his eighteen-month sojourn in Corinth and following a visit to Jerusalem. He was aided significantly by the help of a Jewish-Christian couple from Rome, Priscilla and Aquila.

Luke provides us with a few of the highlights of Paul's ministry there in Acts 19. Following the typical pattern of his missionary outreach, Paul began proclaiming the gospel in the synagogue until opposition to his preaching grew too strong. He then moved to a lecture hall in the city where he taught regularly. The Western text of the book of Acts preserves the tradition that he taught there daily between 11:00 A.M. and 4:00 P.M. Most significantly, Luke claims that not only did people in Ephesus and its environs hear the gospel during these two years, but "all the Jews and Greeks who lived in the province of Asia heard the word of the Lord" (Acts 19:10). It was during this time that churches began in various other cities of western Asia Minor including Colosse, Laodicea, Pergamum, Smyrna, Sardis, Magnesia, Tralles, and elsewhere.

The original church of Ephesus thus consisted of many converted Jews and Gentile God-fearers and sympathizers to the Jewish faith, as well as many Gentiles coming directly from the pagan cults of the city, particularly the cult of Artemis. If the silversmith guild had experienced such a sharp decline of revenues for their images of Artemis, there was probably a sizeable group of Gentiles who embraced the one true God and the Lord Jesus Christ.

It is highly unlikely that the church met as a large group in one central location. Groups of believers probably met in homes every Lord's day in various parts of the city and in the local villages (e.g., Hypaipa, Diashieron, Neikaia, and Koloe).

The Spiritual Climate of the Area

There are some distinctive features of the religious environment of the area that help us better understand the discipleship issues these new believers faced and why Paul addressed certain topics and stressed others in his letter.

A religiously pluralistic environment. Although best known as the sacred home

to the Artemis cult, up to fifty other gods and goddesses were worshiped in Ephesus. Among those worshiped in Ephesus were Zeus, Athena, Aphrodite, Asclepius, Apollo, Dionysus, Demeter, Hekate, Tyche, Theos Hypsistos, Meter Oreia, and Hephaistos.[3] The two Egyptian deities Isis and Sarapis were also popular in the city.[4] There was a spirit of religious tolerance among the people. In fact, people typically worshiped more than one deity.

The pervasive influence of the Artemis cult. Artemis of Ephesus was undeniably the most important deity to the people living in the city. Her relationship to the city was forged in terms of a divinely directed covenant relationship. One month of the year was named after her, Olympic-style games were held in her honor (the Artemisia), and the cult was the major savings and loan institution for the entire region. The temple of Artemis was lauded by ancient writers as one of the seven wonders of the ancient world.[5]

Magic and spirit powers. Ephesus also bore a reputation in antiquity for magic, shamanism, and the occult arts. The practice of magic was predicated on an animistic worldview in which good and evil spirits were involved in practically every area of life. Magic represented a means of harnessing spiritual power through rituals, incantations, and invocations.[6] Luke informs us that many believers gathered their magical books together and burned them after a fear fell on them following Sceva's failed exorcism of a demonized man (Acts 19:17–20). His account demonstrates the difficulty new Christians had in turning completely away from their former practices in the process of discipleship. It would have been tempting for them to continue using magical incantations and invoking other deities and helper spirits for issues in daily life.

A Portrait of the Situation

Paul engaged in his Ephesian ministry in the mid–50s (perhaps A.D. 52–55). During this time the church was established and numerous other churches in a radius from Ephesus were planted. After his abrupt departure from the city precipitated by the silversmiths and adherents

CURETES STREET

(left) At the beginnng of the street, the columns depict Hercules draped in a lion skin.

(right) The well-preserved street passes by the principal civic buildings of Ephesus.

to the Artemis cult, Paul traveled to Macedonia and Greece. From there he went to Jerusalem, where he was arrested (see Acts 20–21). From that point on, Paul was incarcerated by the Romans—in Caesarea and then, after his harrowing sea voyage, in Rome (A.D. 60–62). It is from his imprisonment in the capital city that Paul writes this letter, probably shortly after he writes to the Colossian believers.

In the five years or so since his departure, a lot has happened in the churches of Ephesus and its environs. The believers have continued to proclaim the gospel in the area and many more Gentiles have put their faith in Christ and joined the Christian community. These new believers have never met Paul, but they have certainly heard of him and respected his authority as an apostle of Christ.

Coming to Christ from a background of animism, goddess worship, magical practices, and a variety of other religions, these people need a more extensive grounding in the gospel and its implications for life. Paul writes the letter to support the Ephesian leadership in addressing a variety of concerns. Three issues in particular surface as the most prominent:

1. When these people turned to Christ and joined the community, their fear of evil spirits and demonic powers did not vanish. They would have been greatly tempted to hold onto some of their household idols and their magical texts in spite of the precedent set by the original believers of Ephesus in the historic book-burning episode. These dear believers need reassurance as to the preeminence of Christ in relationship to other spiritual forces and their own access to the power of God for resisting the hostile powers.

2. Because of their immoral pre-Christian lifestyle, they need help and admonishment in cultivating a lifestyle consistent with their salvation in Christ—a lifestyle free from drunkenness, sexual immorality, lying, stealing, bitterness, and many other vices.

3. With a large influx of Gentiles into the Ephesian house churches,

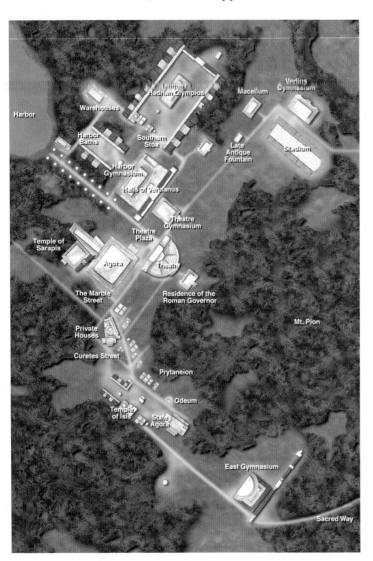

a situation was created for a heightening of tensions between Gentiles and Jews. Not only was there already a natural tension between Jews and Gentiles, but Gentile converts often lacked an appreciation for the Jewish heritage of their new faith.

Paul therefore sets out to write a general letter to the network of house churches in Ephesus and the churches of the region to address these and other issues. There does not appear to be a specific crisis (such as he addressed at Galatia or Corinth), but he nevertheless speaks in a pastoral and apostolic manner to a variety of real needs of which he has become aware through Tychicus and others.

Introduction to the Letter (1:1–2)

Paul, an apostle of Christ Jesus (1:1). Whereas Timothy is named as cowriter of Colossians and Philemon (written just before Ephesians), Paul names himself as the sole author of this letter. It is uncertain if Timothy is still in Rome or has departed to serve in another area. We do know that he becomes a key leader among the churches in Ephesus shortly after this letter is written (see 1 Timothy).

To the saints in Ephesus (1:2). The text of the NIV places a footnote here that reads, "Some early manuscripts do not have *in Ephesus*." There are only six manuscripts that omit Ephesus, but three of these are generally regarded as very reliable (Sinaiticus [Å], Vaticanus [B], and a second-century papyrus [p^{46}]). This has led some scholars to think that Ephesians was not originally written to believers in the city of Ephesus, but rather was a circular letter intended for a number of churches. This is unnecessary, however, because the vast majority of manuscripts and early translations into other languages support the inclusion of "in Ephesus" and also because there is a reasonable explanation for its omission from 1:2 very early. The contents of Ephesians are especially well-suited to a broad readership. It is likely that a scribe deliberately omitted "in Ephesus" for the purpose of the public reading of Scripture in another location (e.g., in Egypt). A similar omission, likely for the same reason, occurs in Romans, where several manuscripts omit "in Rome" in 1:7. Thus, it is probable that the letter was originally addressed by the apostle Paul to believers residing in the third largest city of the Roman empire, Ephesus.

Praise to God For His Remarkable Plan of Redemption (1:3–14)

Paul begins his letter with a poetically crafted exclamation of praise to the Father. The style of this section is quite different from the rest of the letter and has affinities to the Psalms and Jewish hymns that we know from the Dead Sea Scrolls. The language is designed to evoke an attitude of praise and thanksgiving to our great God and Lord. The apostle Paul could not teach theology in a dry and detached way. To reflect on the plan and work of God provoked an emotional response that led him into praise and worship.

This passage speaks of the overall plan of God, conceived before he created the world and now brought into effect by the Lord Jesus Christ. The passage highlights the overall sovereignty of God. His plan is unfolding just as he purposed.

▶ Fate and Astral Powers

People living in Ephesus and western Asia Minor lived in constant dread of astral powers that controlled fate. The Stoic writer Manilius (first century A.D.) writes:

> They [the Egyptian priests] were the first to see, through their art, how fate depends on the wandering stars. Over the course of many centuries they assigned with persistent care to each period of time the events connected with it: the day on which someone is born, the kind of life he shall lead, the influence of every hour on the laws of destiny, and the enormous differences made by small motions . . . . From long

observation it was discovered that the stars control the whole world by mysterious laws, that the world itself moves by an eternal principle, and that we can, by reliable signs, recognize the ups and downs of fate.[A-1]

The beautiful cult statue of the Ephesian Artemis depicts the goddess as wearing the signs of the zodiac as a necklace, expressing that as Queen of Heaven she had the power to break the bonds of fate. Even some Jewish writings from the Roman period display a concern about fate and the spirits associated with the sun, moon, planets, and stars

Praise be to the God and Father of our Lord Jesus Christ (1:3). The term "praise" (*eulogētos*) has often been translated "blessed." Throughout the Old Testament, the people of God responded to him in praise for delivering them from their enemies and for providing salvation. For instance, in response to God's marvelous redemption of Israel from bondage in Egypt, Moses' father-in-law exclaimed, "Praise be to the LORD, who rescued you from the hand of the Egyptians and of Pharaoh, and who rescued

the people from the hand of the Egyptians. Now I know that the LORD is greater than all other gods" (Ex. 18:10–11). Because of his salvation, the psalmist bursts forth in praise: "The LORD lives, and blessed be my rock; And exalted be the God of my salvation" (Ps. 18:46 NASB). Paul cannot contain himself as he ponders the ultimate act of redemption in Christ.

Jesus is named in this verse alongside the Father as both Lord and Messiah. He is the agent of redemption and the focus of God's eternal plan.

[He] has blessed us in the heavenly realms (1:3). Paul conceives of heaven not only as a place where believers will live after they die, but also as a spiritual realm. It is the place where God and the resurrected Christ currently live (1:3, 20; 2:6) as well as where the powers of darkness continue to operate (3:10; 6:12). Because of Christ's work of redemption on the cross and their present relation-

ARTEMIS ADORNED WITH THE ZODIAC

▼

ship with him, believers now have access to spiritual power to aid in their struggle against the evil one.

He chose us in him before the creation of the world (1:4). Paul's teaching here communicates relevant and extraordinary truth about ultimate reality for these believers in Asia. Contrary to popular belief, their fate was not wrapped up in the stars and the planets, but in the one true almighty God, who made the sun and the stars. God had in fact chosen them to be in Christ before he made the heavens and the earth. What a tremendous comfort this teaching must be to new believers still worried about their foul horoscopes or the threat of astral powers to their daily lives.

To be holy and blameless in his sight (1:4). God's purpose for his people has always been for them to become like him in holiness. When he gave the Israelites the law after delivering them from Egypt, he declared, "I am the LORD who brought you up out of Egypt to be your God; therefore be holy, because I am holy" (Lev. 11:45).

Adopted as his sons (1:5). The adoption of a child was a practice that everyone in the Greco-Roman world would have been familiar with. Under Roman law, an adopted child acquired all of the legal rights of a natural born child and lost all rights held in his former family. The child also received the adopting parents' family name and shared in the status of the new family.[7] The most decisive influence on Paul's thought, however, is in the promise of adoption God made to David by Nathan the prophet: "I will be his father, and he will be my son" (2 Sam. 7:14). Jesus himself has fulfilled this

promise as the descendant of David who sits on the throne. By virtue of union with Jesus, believers share in this adoption and truly become children of God.

To the praise of his glorious grace (1:6). Variations of this refrain of praise punctuate this passage at three intervals (1:6, 12, 14). Reflecting on the awesome and gracious plan of God involving Jesus, Paul exults in the same way as the psalmist who exclaimed, "My tongue will speak of your righteousness and of your praises all day long" (Ps. 35:28). (On grace, see comments on 2:7.)

In him we have redemption through his blood (1:7). The people of Israel were once delivered from oppressive slavery to corrupt rulers and taskmasters in Egypt. The Old Testament repeatedly refers to this as Israel's redemption (see Deut. 7:8; 9:26; 13:5). Now God has delivered his people from the much more deadly and enslaving power of sin. He has done this by Christ's sacrificial death on the cross—a costly ransom price. Believers can therefore experience the forgiveness of sins.

He made known to us the mystery of his will (1:9). "Mystery" was a term widely known in the ancient world. Many of the Gentile converts in the Ephesian churches have probably experienced ritual initiation into one or more of the mystery cults, such as the cult of Artemis, Isis, Cybele, or Dionysus. They are called "mysteries" because the adherents were sworn to secrecy about what they experienced. The mystery Paul is talking about here is substantially different from this. He is speaking about God's plan that can only be known through revelation. This same use of the word occurs in the book of Daniel to describe Nebuchad-nezzar's divinely inspired dream about God's plan for the ages.[8] The word Paul uses for "made known" (*gnōrizō*) also occurs in Daniel for God's revelatory activity.[9]

When the times will have reached their fulfillment (1:10). The Greek and Roman world generally thought of time as unending. The world will continue on and on. The Old Testament, by contrast, is clear that time is measured and fixed (see Dan. 9:24–27). At some point in time history as we know it will be drawn to a conclusion. This period of fulfillment will represent the climax of God's redemptive plan.

To bring all things in heaven and on earth together under one head, even Christ (1:10). There has been a significant rupture in God's creation. Angels in heaven have rebelled against the Lord. Sin has emerged as a power that not only enslaves God's creation, but also causes people to revolt against him and his purposes. Paul declares here that this condition will not continue forever. All of creation—both heavenly principalities and every person—will someday be

forced to submit to the righteous and all-powerful reign of the Messiah. All will be brought under the universal "headship" of Jesus. The initial realization of this plan has already taken place in Jesus' incarnation, proclamation of the kingdom, death, and exaltation to the right hand of God. Believers now await the complete fulfillment.

The word of truth, the gospel of your salvation (1:13). First-century Ephesus had nearly fifty gods and goddesses claiming to be true. There were also a wide variety of philosophies that laid claim to providing knowledge of the truth. In this environment, Paul does not shrink back from insisting that the good news of Jesus as the revelation of ultimate reality is *the* truth (the Greek text has the article). This was not just a matter for the satisfaction of intellectual curiosity. Jesus revealed insight into the plight of humanity and their need for deliverance.

You were marked in him with a seal, the promised Holy Spirit (1:13). Seals were used widely in the ancient world as the primary way of indicating ownership. They were typically made of hard stones or precious metals and had a distinctive image engraved on them (usually the representation of a favorite deity, a hero, or a portrait). All of a person's significant possessions were marked with the impression of the seal. Even slaves and livestock were marked by the owner.[10] In some cases, people declared themselves the possession of a deity by the imprint of a seal.[11] The one true God has also marked his possessions by means of a seal, yet his seal does not leave a physical impression. He has given his people the gift of the Holy Spirit as a sign of their belonging to him.

A deposit guaranteeing our inheritance (1:14). The Spirit is also represented as a down payment on the full future inheritance believers will receive. The word *arrabōn*, here translated "a deposit guaranteeing," is familiar to Paul's readers from the context of business and trade. In much the same way that we put a down payment on a car or a home, in the ancient world someone could put a down payment on an item to secure a legal claim on it. Although believers have nothing to offer but themselves, God so values his people that he has put down a deposit and will complete the transaction in the future. The Spirit, then, is a guarantee of the full experience of salvation—the inheritance—that believers have yet to receive.

A Prayer for an Increased Awareness of God's Power (1:15–23)

Following immediately after his sentence of praise, Paul expresses thanksgiving to God for his Asia Minor converts and reports how he and his companions have been interceding for them.

Ever since I heard about your faith (1:15). About five to seven years have passed since Paul was last with the Ephesians. He engaged in further mission work, was arrested in Jerusalem, spent nearly two years in prison in Caesarea, experienced a harrowing voyage and shipwreck on his way to Rome, and is now imprisoned in the capital city. A lot has happened in Asia Minor since he was with them. Nevertheless, he has received word from his coworkers that their faith is growing and their love is abounding. Probably many others have become Christians in this period of time and their

faith is flourishing. For this, Paul gives thanks to God.

The Spirit of wisdom and revelation (1:17). The heart of Paul's request for these dear people is for their knowledge of God to increase. Paul knows that this is not just a matter of intellectual apprehension. The Holy Spirit needs to be operative in their lives to impress the truths about God and his plan of salvation onto their minds and into their hearts.

This is also necessary because "the ruler of the kingdom of the air" is still at work, endeavoring to disrupt what God is doing in the lives of these people. Paul speaks of the work of the Spirit in terms similar to how Isaiah prophesied that the Spirit would work in the Messiah: "The Spirit of the LORD will rest on him—the Spirit of wisdom and understanding, the Spirit of counsel and of power, the Spirit of knowledge and of the fear of the LORD" (Isa. 11:2).

The eyes of your heart (1:18). This is a fascinating (and somewhat humorous) metaphor because hearts do not have eyes, yet the intent is clear. It appears that Paul himself has created this image since it does not appear in any literature prior to him. The closest statement comes from the Dead Sea Scrolls: "May he illuminate your heart with the discernment of life."[12] In the Old Testament and Judaism, "heart" was used metaphorically as the place of a person's intellectual and spiritual life. Paul is here using colorful language to pray for the people to receive a deep-seated awareness of God.

The hope (1:18). This is the first of three specific requests Paul reports praying for the Ephesians. Given their previous background in non-Christian religions largely devoid of future hope as well as their previous deep-seated beliefs about astral fate, this was very important.

His glorious inheritance in the saints (1:18). This is Paul's second request. He has already mentioned the future inheritance of the Ephesians in 1:14, which consists of their hope, but here he speaks of them as *God's* valuable inheritance. The love of God is a significant theme in this letter. How wonderful it must feel to these people, accustomed as they have been to worshiping capricious and self-serving gods and goddesses, now to be in a relationship with a God who dearly loves them and values them as his choice inheritance.

> ## REFLECTIONS
>
> **WHEN GOD LOOKS AT YOU, HE DOES** not shrink back in horror and disgust. He sees a person of inestimable value and beauty. He loves you so much that he gave the costliest gift imaginable to obtain you as his own "glorious" inheritance. You will be his cherished son or daughter forever.

His incomparably great power (1:19). This letter has more to say about power than any of Paul's other letters. His final request is for the Ephesians to be able to grasp the vastness of the one true God's mighty power at work in their lives. Why does he pray for this? Because spiritual power is a huge issue for these people. They are accustomed to seeking spiritual power through their magical practices. Based on Luke's account we know it has been difficult for many of these people to let loose of their magical incantations and

formulas. With language that is emphatic, Paul assures them that God's power is beyond that of any competing spirit power, god, or goddess. Not only do they serve the most powerful God, but he manifests his power in their lives for protection, growth, and service.

Seated him at his right hand (1:20). Jesus not only died for our sins and rose from the dead, but he has been installed at God's right hand on the heavenly throne. This was an important conviction of the early Christians, evidenced in part by the fact that Psalm 110:1—cited here as fulfilled in Christ—is quoted more than any other Old Testament passage by New Testament writers.

The setting of Psalm 110 was the enthronement of a king. The right hand of God occurs frequently in the Old Testament as a way of describing a position of power (see Ex. 15:6) and favor (Ps. 80:17). The enthronement of Christ establishes his identity as the messianic king and highlights his sovereignty over all of creation. The enemies that this victorious king has subjugated are not the Romans or any other physical army, but the spiritual forces of evil.

Far above all rule and authority, power and dominion (1:21). Paul now elaborates on these spiritual enemies by listing a few of them. These labels are just a few of many possible terms Paul could have used to describe demonic spirits. Although these terms do not occur in the Old Testament, they were well known in the Judaism of the time.[13] They had become part of the common vocabulary for spirit powers not only in Judaism, but to some degree also in the Greco-Roman world. The terms may indicate some kind of hierarchy within the demonic realm, but there is no way of determining this. The texts outside of the New Testament that use these terms make no attempt at classifying these angelic powers. Paul uses these words here to convey the fact that these are powerful supernatural forces. They serve to highlight the superiority of Christ because his is "far above" these forces in power and sovereignty.

Every title that can be given (1:21). This phrase (lit., "every name that is named") is loaded with significance for people who have been converted out of a background of participation in magical practices. Discerning and using the names of spirit powers was central to the use of magic. Note the calling of names in lines from three magical papyri:

- "I conjure you by the great names."
- "You, these holy names and these powers, confirm and carry out this perfect enchantment."
- "A phylactery, a bodyguard against demons, against phantasms, against every sickness and suffering, to be written on a leaf of gold or silver or tin or hieratic papyrus. When worn it works mightily, for it is the name of power of the great god and his seal, and it is as follows: . . . [fourteen magical names are given]. . . . These are the names."[14]

Paul wants to assure these new believers they that need not concern themselves with discerning the names of spirit entities or with worrying about some being that may rival Christ in power and authority. There is no conceivable spiritual force outside of the dominion of Christ. The name of Jesus alone, not his name in addition to others, is sufficient for them.

Not only in the present age but also in the one to come (1:21). Paul sees history as divided into two ages—this present evil age and the age to come (see Gal. 1:4). This perspective is one of the standard features of Jewish theology and appears in the book of Daniel. The age to come corresponds to the time when God will restore David's kingdom on the earth.[15]

◀ *left*

NAMING POWERFUL NAMES

Someone wrote the names of five deities on this potsherd (*ostracon*): Sambathis, Artemis, Koura, Dionysus, and Demo.

▶ The Ephesian Names

There is a long tradition of six magical names that was associated with Ephesus: *Askion, Kataskion, Lix, Tetrax, Damnameneus,* and *Aisia.* Known as the "Ephesian Letters" (*Ephesia grammata*), these were the names of six powerful beings who could be called upon for assistance and protection. Plutarch says that the "magi" instructed people who were possessed by evil spirits to repeat to themselves the magic words in order to drive the demons out.[A-2] Even athletes wore the "Ephesian letters" to ensure success.

Head over everything (1:22). The metaphor of headship clearly indicates the sovereignty of Jesus. As the exalted Lord, he possesses ruling authority over everything. Particularly meaningful for the Ephesian readers is the fact that Jesus reigns as supreme over all the supernatural powers that they so deeply feared.

The church, which is his body (1:22–23). Jesus also is "head" in relationship to his "body," which Paul here identifies as the church. Head-body imagery abounded in the ancient world, especially in the medical writers and in some of the philosophers. In these texts, this image stresses a person's function of giving leadership and providing for his people. This image flows naturally out of the observation of human anatomy, where the head coordinates the movements of the members of the body and provides nourishment as well.

The fullness of him who fills everything in every way (1:23). Under the old covenant, God manifested his presence in the temple. The *Shekinah*—the essence, glory, power, and presence of God—filled the temple. Biblical writers could therefore exclaim, "Behold, the house of the Lord is full of his glory."[16] Under the new covenant, God now fills believers directly with his presence through the promised Holy Spirit (Eph. 1:13–14).

This verse also indicates that believers have a mission. God is setting out to fill all of creation with the good news of redemption available in the Messiah Jesus. "In every way" is perhaps better translated "totally" or "in all parts." God manifests his presence in believers so they can move out to reach every corner of the world with the gospel of Christ and then to help each of these new believers grow and mature in every way before God.

The Desperate Human Plight (2:1–3)

From his exultant praise of God and his prayer for the readers, Paul moves to a description of the horrible condition humanity faces: death, slavery, and condemnation. This plight results from the pervasive and powerful influence of evil, which impinges on people in three different but related forms.

The ways of this world (2:2). The literal wording of this phrase is "the age of this world." Paul thereby sets sinful behavior into the context of "this present evil age" (see comments on 1:21). He also speaks of "the world" in a similar way (see 1 Cor. 3:19; 5:10). Paul understands the physical creation and humanity as belonging to the present evil age. The social structures and the value systems of corporate humanity have been corrupted by sin and exert a powerful influence on people.

The ruler of the kingdom of the air (2:2). The second evil influence is the devil, whom Paul describes here as a "ruler"

(*archōn*). This is a common term for human rulers throughout the Greek Old Testament (LXX) as well as documents and inscriptions from the first century. This *archōn* is clearly not a human ruler, but a supernatural power because his domain is "the air" and he is subsequently characterized as a spirit. The Greek text of Daniel also uses this word to refer to angelic powers: the "prince" of Persia and the "prince" of Greece.[17] The Synoptic Gospels describe the devil as "the prince of demons," and John's Gospel terms him "the prince of this world."[18]

The "air" was widely spoken of as the dwelling place of evil spirits in antiquity. One magical papyrus reads: "Protect me from every demon in the air."[19] A Jewish text from the first century also illustrates this belief: "For the person who fears God and loves his neighbor cannot be plagued by the aerial spirit of Beliar since he is sheltered by the fear of God."[20] Satan is here understood, then, to be the ruler of an army of evil spiritual powers who work at promoting disobedience to the purposes of God among humanity.

The cravings of our sinful nature (2:3). This third form of evil influence is literally translated, "the lusts of our flesh." Central to Jewish thinking among the rabbis at the time of Paul was the notion that every person struggled with an inner propensity toward evil. They called this the *yetzer hārāʿ*, "the evil impulse."[21] Paul spoke of this impulse as "the flesh" (*sarx*) and conceived of it as a power welling up from within the person, prompting him or her to act in ways displeasing to God.

The combination of these three evil influences—the world, the devil, and the flesh—exerts a compelling pull on people to sin and transgress God's commandments. People need deliverance and freedom from the overwhelming power of these forces.

We were by nature objects of wrath (2:3). All humanity, having succumbed

EPHESUS
Marble Street.

Ephesians

to the influence of evil, faces the wrath of God for violating his righteous directives. The Old Testament prophets point to a future day, called a "day of wrath," when God will exercise judgment (Zeph. 1:15, 18; 2:2–3). "By nature" reveals that human culpability before God can be attributed to the fact that every person stands in solidarity with Adam, the progenitor of the human race and the first to sin (see Rom. 5:12–14). This resulted in a sinful tendency that spreads like a disease to every single human being.

The Merciful Saving Action of God (2:4–10)

God has responded in his love to the dreadful situation of humanity. He has delivered people from captivity to evil based on the work of Christ. Those who are redeemed are brought into close relationship with Christ and a solidarity with the events of the cross.

His great love for us (2:4). In spite of how undeserving and how unlovely sin-tainted people are, God has a tremendous love for them. This has been true from the beginning. God told Israel: "The LORD did not set his affection on you and choose you because you were more numerous than other peoples, for you were the fewest of all peoples. But it was because the LORD loved you" (Deut. 7:7–8). John's Gospel tells us that it was because God loved the world so much that he sent his Son (John 3:16).

Made us alive with Christ . . . raised us up with Christ . . . and seated us with him (2:5–6). God has brought believers into a relationship with himself through Christ. He has mercifully created a plan whereby people can participate in the

events of the cross—Jesus' death (not explicitly stated here but assumed)—his resurrection, and his ascension/exaltation (see also Rom. 6:4–8). The work of Christ that Paul expresses praise for in chapter 1, he now makes relevant to the plight of believers. This benefit is predicated on entering a relationship of solidarity with Jesus Christ. Not only do people experience forgiveness of sins and life after death, but they presently share in Christ's authority. This is a particularly relevant and important message for these Asia Minor readers who are deeply concerned about how to respond to the unseen world of evil forces.

You have been saved (2:5, 8). No longer are God's people destined for wrath, for they have been saved from this dreadful fate. The experience of salvation goes beyond this future deliverance; it is a present experience based on participation in this past event.

Incomparable riches of his grace (2:7). "Grace" (*charis*) was not a widely used term in Greek philosophical or religious writings, but it was a significant way of describing God's overwhelming love in Jewish circles. It corresponds to the Hebrew word *ḥesed*, which was used commonly in the Old Testament to express the kindness and favor God demonstrated to his people through the covenant.[22] The incredible love of God manifested in the sacrifice of his Son is indeed incomparably great.

Through faith—and this not from yourselves (2:8). A decisive feature of the new covenant that runs counter to many popular misconceptions about divine salvation in Paul's day is that there is nothing a person can do to earn favor with

God. Some Jews, for instance, believed that ultimately the sum total of their works would be weighed on the Judgment Day and God would determine if they had sufficient merit to be saved. This belief is illustrated in one Jewish document that depicts two angels as holding the scales of judgment and recording sins as well as righteous deeds. At the end of time, the aggregate of each person's deeds is tested by fire. The person whose remaining good works outweigh his evil deeds "is justified and the angel of righteousness takes him and carries him up to be saved in the lot of the righteous."[23] Paul here strongly emphasizes that salvation is based entirely on the merits of Christ's work—not ours. We are urged merely to put our faith in Christ.

Created in Christ Jesus to do good works (2:10). The idea that God created people to live righteously and perform good works was well-rooted in Judaism. Rabbi Johanan ben Zakkai (first century A.D.) is reported in the Mishnah to have customarily said, "If thou has wrought much in the Law claim not merit for thyself, for to this end was thou created."[24] Believers in Christ perform these good works based on their relationship with Christ and the power and direction he provides. They do so out of a heart of gratitude for all that Christ has accomplished for them.

The Unity of Jews and Greeks in One Body (2:11–17)

Paul now specifically addresses the Gentiles among his readers. He calls them to remember their former alienation from God and from the Jews. All of that has been changed by the sacrificial death of Christ, who now unites them all into one unified body.

Behind this passage may be a situation of tension between Jewish and Gentile Christians among the house churches of Ephesus and Asia Minor. Perhaps a flood of Gentile new believers entering the churches has led over time to a lack of appreciation for the Jewish heritage of their faith. Note too that throughout the Roman empire a growing anti-Jewish sentiment led to intense flare-ups of racial tension in the cities.

Remember (2:11). God has always called his people to remember their past condition. The intent is not to provoke sorrow, grief, or self-hatred, but to help them appreciate all the more the greatness of God's grace, mercy, and love. The Israelites, for instance, were instructed by God to remember their deliverance from Egypt by an annual feast called "Unleavened Bread": "Then Moses said to the people, 'Commemorate [lit., "remember"] this day, the day you came out of Egypt, out of the land of slavery, because the LORD brought you out of it with a mighty hand. Eat nothing containing yeast'" (Ex. 13:3). The sins and difficulties

EPHESUS
Hadrian's temple.

the Israelites got themselves into could in part be attributed to the fact that "they did not remember" the wondrous works of God and his past acts of deliverance (see Ps. 78:42; 106:7).

You who are Gentiles by birth (2:11). Paul singles out and addresses the non-Jews among the believers in Ephesus. It is important to recognize that Ephesus was a multiethnic city. The reference to Gentiles would include people of many different ethnicities, including Anatolians, Egyptians, Romans, Persians, Syrians, and others.

"Uncircumcised" . . . "the circumcision" (2:11). Jews commonly distinguished themselves from Gentiles by the fact that their males were circumcised—the mark of their covenant with God (Gen. 17:9–14). This became a matter of inappropriate ethnic pride for many Jews, who referred to Gentiles as "the uncircumcision" (lit., "those with foreskins").

Foreigners to the covenants of the promise (2:12). Paul is speaking here of the series of covenants God made with his people: Abraham, Isaac, Jacob/Israel, and David.[25] The singular "promise" is

the Messiah, in whom all of the covenants find their fulfillment. Gentiles have not shared in these covenants nor have they been included in God's special relationship to Israel.

Without God (2:12). There is incredible irony in Paul's referring to a formerly *polytheistic* group of people as "godless" (*atheoi*). What Paul has in mind is the fact that they did not have a relationship with the one true God.

You who once were far away have been brought near (2:13). The language of this verse echoes Isaiah 57:19 ("'Peace, peace, to those far and near,' says the LORD"), which Paul here and more explicitly in Ephesians 2:17 declares as fulfilled by the work of Jesus on the cross. Those "far" are understood to be the Gentiles and those "near" are the Jews. Yet both now have access to the Father only through the blood of Christ.

He himself is our peace (2:14). Peace is found in a person—the Lord Jesus Christ. He is truly the "Prince of Peace" (Isa. 9:6) and has established a kingdom that is characterized by "peace" (Isa. 9:7). Yet it was his sacrifice of himself that serves as the source of this peace. Isaiah prophesied of the Servant of the Lord: "The punishment that brought us peace was upon him, and by his wounds we are healed" (Isa. 53:5). The peace Jesus makes possible is first and foremost with the Father. But this peace extends to human relationship within the body of Christ.

The barrier, the dividing wall of hostility (2:14). Gentiles were allowed to enter the temple enclosure in Jerusalem. This large paved area surrounding the

WARNING INSCRIPTION

A first-century inscription from the balustrade around the Jerusalem temple warning Gentiles not to enter on the pain of death.

▼

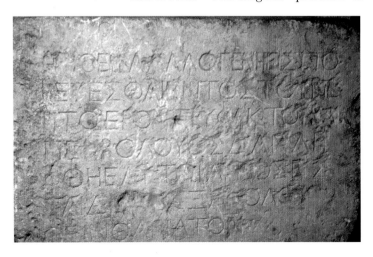

temple and its inner courts was itself enclosed by a double colonnade of pillars standing thirty-seven feet high. The perimeter of this area measured nearly three-quarters of a mile. This outer court was also called the Court of the Gentiles. Gentiles were not allowed access to the inner courts or the temple. A four and a half foot high barrier surrounding the inner courts served as a dividing wall.

The Jewish historian Josephus informs us that thirteen stone slabs written in Greek and Latin stood at intervals on the barrier, warning Gentiles not to enter.[26] Archaeologists have discovered two of these tablets.[27] The inscription reads: "No foreigner is to enter within the forecourt and the balustrade around the sanctuary. Whoever is caught will have himself to blame for his subsequent death."[28] The fact of this barrier recently impressed itself upon Paul's mind because he was falsely accused in Jerusalem for taking a Gentile, Trophimus, into the temple (Acts 21:28–29). This was the reason for his initial imprisonment in Jerusalem and then Caesarea.

Paul's language in this verse appears to make allusion to this barrier—a symbol of the alienation of Gentiles from the Jewish people, from citizenship in Israel, from the promises of the covenants, and, more important, from access to the one true God. Paul declares that the barriers separating Gentiles from God and from Jews have now been destroyed. The physical balustrade at the temple still stood (until the temple was destroyed in A.D. 70), but there is no longer any fence prohibiting direct access to God.

The law with its commandments and regulations (2:15). By his death on the cross, Jesus has fulfilled the law and thus brought to an end the ceremonies and rituals associated with the temple. No longer are the bloody sacrifices, ritual purity, and circumcision essential for the worship of God.

In this one body to reconcile both of them to God (2:16). The word "reconciliation" was widely used in the Greek-speaking world to describe the restoration of a relationship after some kind of rupture through hostility or displeasure. God has not only brought about the possibility of a close relationship with himself, but between two groups formerly at enmity with one another. This does not take place in society at large, but within the church.

We both have access to the Father (2:18). Access to the Father is no longer through the temple priesthood or based on being a Jew. Gentiles and Jews alike now gain direct access to God through the work of Christ and by the indwelling Spirit, the very presence of God with his people.

REFLECTIONS

CHRIST HAS NOT ONLY OVERCOME the divisions separating Jews from Gentiles, but also every barrier that separates people from one another today. This includes race, social status, denominations, and every other dividing wall that we may choose to erect. Our churches should showcase to the world the unifying power of the gospel. How is your church doing? Do you harbor any pride, bitterness, or animosity toward other believers in your heart? The gospel demands that we work toward unity.

God's Citizens, Family, and Temple Indwelt by the Spirit (2:19–22)

Paul now uses three images well known to the people of that time to describe the nature of the church: fellow citizens of a kingdom, members of a family, and a temple.

Fellow citizens (2:19). The background of the word (*politeia*) Paul uses here (as also in 2:12) is in Greek texts that refer to a government, state, or a commonwealth. It never appears in the LXX, although it is used in Judaism leading up to the time of Christ. It is reminiscent of the "kingdom" language used by Jesus. The principal idea is that believers have gained a new citizenship (see Phil. 3:20) in a divinely constituted commonwealth. This is not a private matter, but a corporate experience, in that they join a group of other believers.

Members of God's household (2:19). Paul moves from the image of citizenship to the image of family (see also Gal. 6:10 and 1 Tim. 5:8, where the same Greek word is used). The picture of the "household" conveys a deeper level of intimacy and belonging. Central to the idea of the church is the creation of strong and supportive relationships.

Built on the foundation of the apostles and prophets (2:20). Now Paul begins to develop a picture of the church as a building under construction. The foundation for this building was laid in the first century with the initial leadership of the church. The "apostles" are those directly commissioned by the Lord Jesus and sent by him to plant churches and root them deeply in his word. These include primarily the Twelve and Paul. The "prophets" are not the Old Testament prophets such as Isaiah and Jeremiah, but the New Testament prophets, who were inspired by the Spirit, gave direction and encouragement to the church, and provided leadership (see the leadership role of the prophets in Antioch in Acts 13:1–3).

The chief cornerstone (2:20). The most significant part of the foundation of any large building was the cornerstone. This stone bore much of the weight of the building. Archaeologists have recently discovered five enormous building stones that helped form the foundation of the Jerusalem temple. The largest stone measures fifty-five feet long, eleven feet high, and fourteen feet wide and is estimated to weigh 570 tons.[29] The prophet Isaiah spoke of the importance of the cornerstone in a passage understood in both Judaism and early Christianity as referring to the Messiah: "See, I lay a stone in Zion, a tested stone, a precious cornerstone for a sure foundation; the one who trusts will never be dismayed" (Isa. 28:16). In his development of the image of the church as a temple, Paul presents Jesus as this significant cornerstone. The whole building is established on him,

LARGE FOUNDATION STONES OF THE JERUSALEM TEMPLE

▼

◀

A model of the temple and its courts. The court of women is in the foreground.

including the foundation laid by the apostles and the prophets.

A holy temple (2:21). The Jerusalem temple provided a fitting analogy to the church. It was the place where God manifested his presence to the people of Israel. The Jerusalem temple of Paul's day was also a long time in the making. Josephus informs us that construction on Herod's temple began around 20 B.C. and work on

the temple precincts was not completed until the early 60s.[30] In other words, work is still continuing as Paul writes this letter. God is finished, however, with the physical temple in Jerusalem. He is replacing it with a "temple" comprised of people filled with his Spirit. This temple is also still under construction. People are being added to it, and they are being crafted and refashioned by God to reflect his holiness and purity.

▲

THE ARTEMIS TEMPLE

The scant remains of the ancient temple.

Paul's Apostolic Ministry (3:1–13)

Paul begins to relate to these Asia Minor believers how he has been praying for them, but he abruptly digresses and explains the nature of his ministry as an apostle.

The prisoner of Christ Jesus (3:1). For the first time in this letter, Paul makes explicit reference to the fact that he is incarcerated. He was arrested and is awaiting trial because of his ministry for the cause of Christ.

The administration of God's grace that was given to me (3:2). "Administration" (*oikonomia*) is a colorful word taken from the management of everyday affairs of life in a household (*oikos*). The administrator (*oikonomos*) was a person who managed an estate in accordance with the wishes of the owner (see Luke 16:2–4). Paul compares himself to this domestic official who has been entrusted with a significant responsibility and will ultimately be called to account by the owner. Paul sees himself as a steward of the grace of God manifested in his marvelous plan of salvation.

As I have already written briefly (3:3). Paul is not speaking of a different letter, but what he has already written up to this point.

The mystery of Christ (3:4). "Mystery," as we have already noted in 1:9, is God's plan for the ages that cannot be known apart from revelation. God has revealed his plan of salvation to Paul, the heart and essence of which is Christ, the Messiah. Because Christ is *the* mystery, the definitive revelation of the one true God, the

readers can forsake all of their pseudo-mysteries—the rituals of the gods and goddesses they have worshiped all of their lives.

This mystery is that through the gospel the Gentiles are heirs together . . . members together . . . and sharers together (3:6). The center point of God's plan of salvation is Christ, but he has unfolded the plan of salvation in a way that the people of Israel could not previously discern. God has brought Jews and Gentiles together into one corporate entity, dynamically united to Christ. The threefold stress on "together" brings out that this obliteration of any distinctions is the radical change in God's way of bringing salvation to people. God's people will now be identified based on a dynamic relationship with the risen Christ and their togetherness in a multiethnic and loving group, not by circumcision, ritual purity, and bloody sacrifices.

I became a servant of this gospel (3:7). Consistent with the image of himself as a manager of a household (3:2), Paul now characterizes his ministry as that of a "servant" (*diakovos*), who is under orders from his master (cf. 6:5–9). Paul thereby once again deflects any praise he might receive and points people to Christ.

The manifold wisdom of God should be made known to the rulers and authorities in the heavenly realms (3:10). The evil principalities and powers had tried to thwart God's plan of redemption by inspiring human rulers to put the Messiah to death.[31] They profoundly underestimated the incredible wisdom of God because it was by Jesus' sacrificial death on the cross that God can now forgive the sins of humanity and thereby take away the power of Satan to justly accuse. Jews and Gentiles, formerly held in slavery by the "elemental spirits of the world," have now been redeemed (Gal. 4:3–5 NRSV). The very existence of the church provides a constant witness to the evil angelic realm of God's extraordinary wisdom.

In him we may approach God with freedom and confidence (3:12). The sentence can more literally be translated, "in him we have the freedom [or boldness] and access in confidence." The "freedom/boldness" (*parrēsia*) that Paul speaks of here was common in Greek literature for describing the kind of communication that would occur among close friends. One may address a friend openly, frankly, and confidently. "Access" (*prosagōgē*) is now repeated from 2:18. Believers not only have the right to approach God, but they can approach him with candidness and freedom, much as one would address a close friend.

Prayer for a Deeper Experience of God's Power (3:14–21)

Paul now resumes his prayer request for the Ephesians. He tells these dear believers that he has been praying for a profound realization of the power of God in their lives. This request builds on what he prayed in chapter 1, where the focus was more on gaining an awareness of God's great power available to them. He concludes his prayer with a beautiful doxology—an ascription of praise to God.

I kneel before the Father (3:14). This is one of the few times that Paul describes his posture in prayer. Kneeling was a symbol of deep respect for the person addressed. The man with leprosy paid Jesus this respect when he knelt before

him and asked for healing.[32] Paul knelt on the beach and prayed with the leaders of the Ephesian church the last time he saw them. When Jesus prayed he often stood and looked into the sky (see Mark 7:34; John 17:1).

From whom his whole family in heaven and on earth derives its name (3:15). This unusual description of God characterizes him as the source of all life. The bestowing of a name means the granting of power and authority. God has made the whole of humanity in all of its diversity. He is also the creator of the heavenly angelic realm—in all its diversity in authorities and roles. In spite of the fact that part of the angelic realm has rebelled against him, God remains sovereign; he is the One who has granted them life and power. This should bring reassurance to people who fear that hostile powers might disrupt what has been asked for them in prayer.

He may strengthen you with power through his Spirit (3:16). The emphasis on the Holy Spirit as the agent for dispensing God's power stands in rather

EPHESUS

The marketplace (*agora*).

stark contrast to the religious climate of the area. In the Greco-Roman world, power was often seen as an impersonal force (like electricity) that could be manipulated, harnessed, or controlled. The power of God comes to his people by means of a *relationship*—a relationship with God by virtue of union with the exalted Christ and with the Holy Spirit residing in each believer.

In your inner being (3:16). The "inner being" is another way of referring to the heart. Paul understands the inner being to be that part of the self in conflict with the power of sin (see Rom. 7:22–23). When personified as a power, sin stands for the three evil influences Paul has already described in Ephesians 2:1–3: the world, the flesh, and the devil. Paul knows very well that believers cannot resist these overwhelmingly powerful evil influences in their own strength.

That Christ may dwell in your hearts through faith (3:17). These people have already received Christ into their lives. Paul is therefore not praying that they will become Christians, but that they will grow in their Christian lives. He prays that Christ will increasingly manifest his reign over every area of their lives and push back the footholds that evil has maintained.

Being rooted and established in love (3:17). Paul mixes metaphors here by combining an agricultural image (a plant taking root) with a construction image (a foundation laid for a building). The net result is an emphasis on love as the primary feature of the Christian life and experience. He subsequently prays, with irony, that believers will come to know something that cannot be fully known—the incredible love of Christ. Love was not a virtue that characterized the workings of the gods and goddesses in the various cults of Asia Minor.

How wide and long and high and deep is the love of Christ (3:18). "The love of Christ" is not in the Greek text. It is a matter of interpretation to decide what the object of the four dimensional terms are. Most commentators have suggested that it is "love" because of the emphasis on love in the surrounding context. A case could be made, however, that this is a reference to the vastness of the power of God. Surprisingly, the only other time that these four words appear together in the Greek language is in a magical text where they speak of the great power of another deity.[33] The readers may well have been familiar with this expression as a way of extolling the power of a god.

Such an interpretation does not diminish the emphasis on love in the passage, but it couples the love of God with his vast power. Love alone is insufficient for God to fulfill his eternal intent for the salvation of humanity. He needs the power and ability to carry it out. Such an emphasis on the cosmic scope of God's power fits with the emphasis of the

---

REFLECTIONS

DOES JESUS "LIVE IN YOUR HEART"?

How much of it? What areas of your life are still largely determined by self-centeredness, unhealthy influences, and sinful ideas? Progress in the Christian life only comes through allowing Jesus to fill you with his powerful and loving presence to resist sin and cultivate a selfless love.

prayer in Ephesians 1 on the surpassing greatness of his power and the concerns of Paul's readers, who continue to entertain questions about the power of the gods, goddesses, and spirits they formerly worshiped.

To him who is able to do immeasurably more than all we ask or imagine (3:20). In an emotive outburst of praise at the conclusion of the prayer, Paul once again highlights the superabundance of God's power. The overt emphasis on the enabling power of God here and throughout the letter likely comes to expression because Paul is addressing a group of believers on the nature of the Christian life in light of the continuing presence and hostility of the evil principalities and powers. This is a deep concern for Christians in Ephesus and Asia Minor because of the widespread influence of magic, the mysteries of underworld deities, and astrology.

Call to Unity (4:1–6)

The Lord wants his people to live together in harmony. Yet this is not a tolerance of anything. Paul has warned the Ephesian elders a few years earlier that "men will arise and distort the truth in order to draw away disciples after them" (Acts 20:30). Paul calls these people to live and work together in a unity that flows out of Christlike attitudes and a common core of beliefs.

As a prisoner of the Lord (4:1). Paul begins his appeal to unity with a reminder that he is held by chains in Rome. There is irony in the fact that the political structure known for peace (*pax romana*, "the peace of Rome") imprisoned a man for proclaiming the gospel of peace. Paul saw his true Lord as Jesus and not the Roman emperor.

I urge you (4:1). This expression actually stands first in the Greek text and marks the beginning of the second half of his letter. Paul appeals to these new believers to bring their behavior into conformity with the pure and righteous God whom they now serve.

To live a life worthy (4:1). The literal wording behind "to live" is "to walk." Throughout the Old Testament and in Jewish literature, "walking" was used to describe how a person conducted one's life. When he appealed to God to prolong his life, Hezekiah prayed, "Remember, O LORD, how I have walked before you faithfully and with wholehearted devotion and have done what is good in your eyes" (2 Kings 20:3). In Jewish tradition, *Halakah* (from the Hebrew word *hlk*, "to walk") was the set of laws and traditions governing daily life.

Humble ... gentle ... patient (4:2). These virtues give practical help toward the goal of maintaining unity among believers. Although Gentile philosophers and moral teachers sometimes spoke of the importance of "gentleness," they rarely, if ever, extolled "humility" and "patience." Throughout the Old Testament, God tells his people how he wants for them to have a spirit of brokenness before him (see Ps. 34:18; Isa. 66:2). The Lord Jesus himself begins his Sermon on the Mount with a call to humility (see Matt. 5:3–5): "Blessed are the poor in spirit, for theirs is the kingdom of heaven."

Make every effort to keep (4:3). Paul does not urge believers to keep working toward an ideal of unity. He assumes that it is already there by virtue of believers sharing a common experience of being united by one Spirit. The task for believers is to preserve the unity that God has given his people.

The bond of peace (4:3). Paul represents the peace that Christ supplies as a chain that ties people together. This idea may have come to Paul as he considered the way his chains bound him to his guard.

One . . . one . . . (4:4–6). The word "one" appears seven times in these three verses. The basis for unity is found in the common core of beliefs of the one church Jesus has created.

REFLECTIONS

UNITY IS IMPORTANT, BUT NOT AT any cost. This is why Paul follows his exhortation with a confession of faith. Church unity needs to be rooted in a shared commitment to the essentials of the faith. The problem we often face is in allowing personality conflicts and disputes over nonessentials to shatter the bond of peace.

One Spirit (4:4). Non-Christians living in this environment believed in many different spirits and were accustomed to making distinctions between helpful and harmful spirits. Paul is not denying the reality of the spirit realm by saying that there is only one Spirit. Rather, he is placing emphasis on the one true Spirit from God, who joins believers to the one body of Christ and indwells their lives. This is the only Spirit that they should concern themselves with now.

Who is over all and through all and in all (4:6). God, who is "over all," is sovereign over heaven, earth, and all the so-called gods and goddesses. Although on the surface, "through all and in all" may appear to be a pantheistic notion of God (he is in everything), this expression stops short of affirming the pantheistic notion of "the one God *is* the all." The wording is rooted in the Old Testament statements about the omnipotence of God over all creation (e.g., Isa. 6:3, "the whole earth is full of his glory"; see also Ps. 8:6–9).

Each Member Contributes to the Growth of the Body (4:7–16)

Jesus himself is powerfully at work in the new community uniting it, strengthening it, and enabling it to appropriate Christian virtues and resist evil influences from the world. By virtue of his exaltation to the right hand of God, Christ has bestowed spiritual giftings on his people.

To each one of us grace has been given (4:7). Whereas Paul speaks of spiritual gifts (*charismata*) in 1 Corinthians and Romans, here he refers to a special grace (*charis*) each believer receives. He created the word *charismata* on the basis of *charis* as a way of referring to the varied and specific manifestations of God's grace to each individual for serving others in the body of Christ.

This is why it says, "When he ascended on high" (4:8). As a lead-in to his discussion about spiritually gifted people, Paul cites Psalm 68:18. This is appropriate because the original setting of this psalm celebrates God's triumphant ascent of Mount Zion after delivering his people (through his earthly king). In appropriating this psalm, Paul sees Jesus as the victorious king who has vanquished his enemies through his death on the cross and his resurrection. As the victor, he now provides gifts to his people.

He led captives in his train (4:8). The captives Jesus led were the evil principalities and powers. Colossians 2:15 uses the imagery of a Roman triumphal procession to describe Jesus' victory over them by means of the cross.

[He] gave gifts to men (4:8). This passage differs from the Hebrew and Greek versions of Psalm 68:18, which read, "You received gifts from men." Paul here appears to be citing an early Aramaic version of the psalm (preserved in a Targum—a written Aramaic translation of the Old Testament) that contains "he gave." The Targum interprets the giving as a reference to Moses' giving of the law.[34]

What makes Psalm 68 all the more significant to this context is that Jews were accustomed to hearing this passage read aloud each year in their synagogues at Pentecost as a designated reading for the day. The law of Moses is no longer to be seen as the focal point and fulfillment of this psalm, but rather the incarnation (descent) and resurrection/exaltation (ascent) of Christ.

Because of Christ's ascent to the right hand of God, he could send the Holy Spirit at Pentecost to incorporate believers into the body of Christ and endow them with special abilities for the building up of the body.

He also descended to the lower, earthly regions (4:9). Although some think this refers to Christ's incarnation or his coming in the presence of the Spirit at Pentecost, it is best to understand this as a reference to the underworld (or, Hades). Christ went there following his death on the cross to proclaim his victory to the imprisoned powers of darkness (1 Peter 3:19). When Christ returns to earth, every knee will bow before him of those

"in heaven and on earth *and under the earth*" (Phil. 2:10, italics added).

Pastors and teachers (4:11). In addition to the apostles, prophets, and evangelists, God gives the church pastors and teachers. The two terms stand under the same article in the Greek text and should therefore be seen as two functions of the same gifted person: a pastor/teacher. Surprisingly, this is the only time that Paul uses the word "pastor" in the New Testament. In the common language of the day, a "pastor" was a sheepherder. Jesus applied this image to himself in John 10, when he spoke of himself as "the good shepherd" (John 10:11). Paul now takes the image and applies it to those who lead and teach in the body of Christ.

To prepare God's people for works of service (4:12). The gifted leaders of the church are called primarily to help prepare the various members of Christ's body to serve one another with the overall goal of assisting each person to know Christ better and reflect his character in their lives.

Tossed back and forth by the waves (4:14). A boat in the middle of a tempest in the Mediterranean Sea was unstable and out of control—as Paul knew so well in his recent dramatic voyage to Rome. Believers not sufficiently grounded in the teachings of the Scripture and in a solid relationship with Christ are easy prey for deceitful teachers.

Every wind of teaching (4:14). Various kinds of false teachings constantly threatened the churches that Paul planted (see also Acts 20:29–30). Paul does not appear to have a specific false teaching in mind here; rather, he is seeking to immunize the Ephesians from those who will assuredly come.

The whole body, joined and held together by every supporting ligament (4:16). The proper functioning of the church is comparable to the human body. The head provides leadership, direction, and guidance to the body, but it is essential for every supporting ligament to do its part. The terminology Paul uses here for this elaborate metaphor has its roots in the medical language of the day (as can be seen in Galen, a doctor who lived in Pergamum). The image highlights the unity of the church, but also the fact that God empowers each member to contribute to the overall edification of the entire body.[35]

▶ Some False Teachings That Threatened the Churches

- **Judaizing Influences**—a group of Jewish Christians that told the Galatians they needed to be circumcised and obey certain features of the Jewish law to be saved.
- **Syncretistic Teachings**—a faction in the Colossian church that mixed Christianity with local folk beliefs.
- **Docetism**—in subsequent years at Ephesus, a faction that surfaced within the church proclaiming that Jesus did not really come in the flesh.
- **Gnosticism**—late in the first century and throughout the second, a heresy that became a serious threat to the churches in Asia Minor.

Developing a Distinctively Christian Lifestyle (4:17–24)

Christ leads his people into a different lifestyle from the environment that surrounds them.

You must no longer live as the Gentiles do (4:17). Paul makes it clear that these believers must make a clean break with the patterns of thinking and behavior that characterized their lives before they became followers of Christ. He focuses particularly on the Gentile believers because they have come from a background of worshiping false deities and leading immoral lives.

In the futility of their thinking (4:17). Jewish wisdom tradition of Paul's time viewed Gentiles as utterly foolish in the way they ignored the signs of the one true God in creation. Much of Paul's language here and in Romans 1:21–24 reflects Wisdom of Solomon 13:1: "For all people who were ignorant of God were foolish by nature; and they were unable from the good things that are seen to know the one who exists." Their empty and darkened thinking has resulted in estrangement from their Creator and the Source of all life.

The hardening of their hearts (4:18). In the Old Testament, a heart was said to be "hardened" when the will and thinking of a person had become insensitive to God and actually withstood him. "Hardness" is used repeatedly in Exodus to describe the condition of Pharaoh's heart—he hardens his own heart (e.g., Ex. 7:13, 22; 8:19; 9:35) and ultimately God hardens it (e.g., 4:21; 7:3; 14:4).

They have given themselves over to sensuality (4:19). Paul places the miserable condition of these Gentile sinners squarely on their own shoulders. They have immersed themselves in an undisciplined lifestyle of gratifying every self-oriented and unholy pleasure.

Indulge in every kind of impurity (4:19). Jews in the first century were deeply concerned about ceremonial purity—avoiding "common" or unclean foods, not touching a corpse, and keeping a variety of other purity regulations based on the Mosaic law and Jewish tradition. Paul, however, stresses only the importance of moral purity for followers of Christ. He insists that all his churches renounce the various kinds of moral impurities that were so rampant in the culture in which they lived.

You were taught . . . to put off your old self . . . and put on the new self (4:22–24). Paul calls these believers to a transformed life. He roots this in the fact that God has bestowed on them a new life in the Spirit—they possess a new self, a new identity. As a way of expressing the struggle between the new and the old, Paul uses the imagery of taking off and putting on clothing, a picture anyone in the ancient world—or now—can understand.

In Romans, Paul spoke of clothing oneself with the Lord Jesus Christ and not gratifying the desires of the evil inclination (i.e., the flesh) (Rom. 13:14). The same idea is present here. When someone becomes a Christian, that person is supernaturally transformed by entering a close relationship with Jesus Christ. Nevertheless, sinful tendencies remain present and believers must become in their daily lives what they truly already are in Christ. Paul urges them to get rid of sinful practices and practice virtuous behavior instead.

Being corrupted . . . made new (4:22–23). There is no middle ground of neutrality in the Christian life. Either one is succumbing to the powerful influences that cause moral corruption or one is being empowered by the Lord to appropriate righteous and pure attitudes and behavior.

Specific Moral Exhortations (4:25–5:2)

In the next portion of his letter, Paul gives concrete examples of where this renewing activity needs to take place in the lives of these Asia Minor believers. Most of these exhortations have to do with the area of social relationships. People today sometimes overglamorize the life of the early church. This passage helps bring us back to reality. The believers in these house churches struggle with lying, anger, stealing, dirty talk, hard feelings, and even bitterness. There is nothing here that is unique to the churches of Asia Minor. These are tendencies that Christians everywhere have had to deal with.

Do not let the sun go down while you are still angry (4:26). The Old Testament designates sunset as the time limit for a number of items, such as paying the wages of a day laborer (Deut. 24:15). Throughout the Old and New Testaments, anger is viewed as something to be avoided, if at all possible. James, for example, urges believers to "be slow to become angry."[36] The quotation from Psalm 4:4 used here in Ephesians 4:28 does not give permission to vent anger, but cautions that when it comes, one should get a handle on it quickly.

Jewish tradition, as expressed in the Dead Sea Scrolls, encouraged community members not to let anger spill over into the next day in any case of discipline: "They shall rebuke each man his brother according to the commandment and shall bear no rancor from one day to the next" (CD 7:2–3).[37] Even non-Christian Greeks living in the first century understood the danger of allowing anger to continue unabated—even overnight. Plutarch writes, "We should next pattern ourselves after the Pythagoreans, who,

▶
EPHESUS

The Arcadian Way
leading from the
harbor to the
theater.

though related not at all by birth, yet sharing a common discipline, if ever they were led by anger into recrimination, never let the sun go down before they joined right hands, embraced each other, and were reconciled."[38]

Do not give the devil a foothold (4:27). The term "foothold" (*topos*) could refer to a "chance" or "opportunity," but in line with the use of spatial language throughout Ephesians it is probably better to understand it in the sense of "space" for the operation of an evil spirit. The same word appears in the teaching of Jesus to refer to a spirit looking for a place to go: "When an evil spirit comes out of a man, it goes through arid places seeking rest [*topos*, i.e., a resting place] and does not find it. Then it says, 'I will return to the house I left'" (Luke 11:24). First-century Judaism saw anger as a magnet that attracts the working of an evil spirit: "Anger and falsehood together are a double-edged evil, and work together to perturb the reason. And when the soul is continually perturbed, the Lord withdraws from it and Beliar rules it."[39]

Do not grieve the Holy Spirit of God (4:30). The Holy Spirit does not leave a believer, but the Spirit may be grieved by sinful behavior and what influence the Spirit had is quenched (cf. 1 Thess. 5:19).

Live a life of love, just as Christ loved us and gave himself up for us (5:2). The high point and foundation of all Christian ethics is love, patterned on the example of Christ's sacrificial death. While it is true that the Greek word *agapaō* is used in this passage (versus *eroō* or *phileō*) there is no example of this magnitude of love in all of Greek literature.

It is not the word that is important, it is the example.

Darkness and Light (5:3–14)

But among you there must not be even a hint of sexual immorality (5:3). Sexual immorality (Paul here uses the word *porneia*) was an enormous problem in the early church among the Gentiles. Adulterous relationships, men sleeping with their slave girls, incest, prostitution, "sacred" sexual encounters in the local temples, and homosexuality were all a part of everyday life in that culture. There was no pervasive social standard with regard to sexual relations. Jews had long been appalled at the behavior of the Gentiles in this regard and considered them "impure." The Mishnah even prohibits a Jewish woman from ever being left alone with a Gentile because he cannot be trusted sexually.[40] The word *porneia* is a broad term covering all kinds of illicit sexual behavior, not just fornication or premarital sex. The term is used abundantly in Jewish literature written in Greek with reference to sexual sin of all kinds.[41]

Obscenity, foolish talk, or coarse joking (5:4). Not only are Christians called to a high standard of sexual purity, they are urged not to cheapen and demean sexuality by making it the topic of crude

REFLECTIONS

TELEVISION TALK SHOWS, SIT-COMS, and call-in radio have majored in the kind of coarse humor that Paul cautions us to avoid. Our "old selves" are drawn to this form of entertainment, but it is destructive to our souls.

jokes, as so often happened in Gentile society. Paul uses three colorful words here—not found in the Old Testament, but from the context of Gentile moral exhortation. The only proper way to respond to God for sexuality is to practice it in the right context and give thanks to him for this wonderful gift.

Such a man is an idolater (5:5). Ephesus and its environs abounded with idolatry—the worship of the images of gods and goddesses in place of the one true God. Here Paul takes idolatry a step further by associating it with sexual immorality and the greedy pursuit of wealth. This is not an innovation with Paul, for other Jewish writers had made this connection: "My children, love of money leads to idolatry, because once they are led astray by money, they designate as gods those who are not gods";[42] "The sin of promiscuity is the pitfall of life, separating man from God and leading on toward idolatry, because it is the deceiver of the mind and the perceptions."[43] Philo sharply criticized the "money lovers" who would "procure gold and silver coins from every side and treasure their hoard like a divine image in a sanctuary, believing it to be a source of blessing and happiness of every kind."[44]

Let no one deceive you with empty words (5:6). Paul is not thinking here of a group of heretics, but simply of unbelievers who attempt to justify their immoral behavior and pull these new Christians back into an improper lifestyle.

You were once darkness but now you are light (5:8). Darkness and light were images commonly used in all ancient religions. The image is especially prominent in an entire document of the Dead Sea Scrolls that speaks of an impending end-time battle between "the sons of light" (the faithful covenant people of God) and "the sons of darkness" (the devil, his angels, and all of God's human enemies).

Paul shows frequent indebtedness to the book of Isaiah, however, and light-darkness imagery is also prominent there. The Lord says through the prophet: "Arise, shine, for your light has come. . . . See, darkness covers the earth and thick darkness is over the peoples, but the LORD rises upon you and his glory appears over you. . . . The LORD will be your everlasting light" (Isa. 60:1–2, 19). Paul describes one's coming to Christ as a radical change of identity—from darkness to light, from the kingdom of darkness to the kingdom of light. There are echoes here of the teaching of Jesus as represented in John's Gospel: "I am the light of the world. Whoever follows me will never walk in darkness, but will have the light of life" (John 8:12).

"Wake up, O sleeper, rise from the dead, and Christ will shine on you" (5:14).

Paul introduces this quotation in the same way he introduces a citation from the Old Testament (see 4:8), yet this is not a verse from the Old Testament. What is he then quoting? Most likely he is citing oral tradition that was passed on in the early church—here from the context of Christian worship and exhortation.[45] Unfortunately, we have no means of verifying this conclusion since no written texts of first-century Christian liturgy have survived (if they were ever even written down). The essence of this passage is to admonish believers to be morally vigilant and deal with the problem of sin, receiving the grace of Christ to help them in their struggle.

Wise and Spirit-Filled Living (5:15–20)

As wise (5:15). Paul commends to these believers the vast Old Testament teaching about wisdom, especially as represented by the books of Proverbs and Ecclesiastes. There they can find ethical insight into God's will.

Do not get drunk on wine (5:18). Wine and drunkenness were central features of the worship of Dionysus (also known as Bacchus).[46] In the frenzied and ecstatic Dionysiac rituals, intoxication with wine was tantamount to being filled with the spirit of Dionysus. It is therefore conceivable that some of the new believers in Asia Minor were carrying this form of worship with them into the church by associating wine with the filling of the Holy Spirit. Paul repudiates such a notion by denouncing drunkenness and associating the filling of the Spirit with other activities. The problem of drunkenness, however, went far beyond the practices of one cult. It was a societal problem.

Paul's comments on drunkenness denounce intoxication for any reason.

Be filled with the Spirit (5:18). The coming and presence of the Holy Spirit fulfill the Old Testament promise concerning the new covenant and the future messianic age of blessing.[47] The followers of Jesus were "filled with the Holy Spirit" on the day of Pentecost (Acts 2:4), and Peter proclaimed this as the fulfillment of expectation. The Spirit is constantly present with believers, but Paul here urges a regular appropriation of the Spirit's power. The following context suggests some of the means by which believers receive a fuller manifestation of the Spirit's presence in their lives.

◀

DIONYSUS

The god is leaning on a satyr while holding a column adorned with grapes and the god Pan. Cupids are at his feet.

Psalms, hymns, and spiritual songs (5:19). The three terms that Paul chooses here—*psalmos, hymnos,* and *ōdē*—stress the variety of forms of music in the early church. All three words occur in the LXX of Psalms, but *psalmos* is particularly at home in a Jewish context. *Hymnos* was a term used extensively by Gentiles in their pagan worship; they were accustomed to singing *hymnoi* in praise of their gods and goddesses. There are many papyrus examples of hymns sung in honor of Isis, Asclepius, "The Great Mother," Apollo, and many other deities. Verses of hymns were sung every morning at the entrance of the temple of Asclepius. Choruses of hymn singers customarily sang words of praise to Apollo at his temple at Claros, just north of Ephesus.[48] For Christians, it is not the musical form that is important, it is the object

of worship. Christians worship the one true God and the Lord Jesus Christ.

Husbands and Wives (5:21–33)

This passage marks the beginning of a set of instructions to various members of the Christian household (see "Household Duties" at 1 Peter 2:11). Paul addresses husbands and wives, parents and children, and slaves and masters. His most extensive remarks have to do with marriage. Male and female relationships fell far short of the mark of God's ideal in antiquity.

Submit to one another. . . . Wives, submit to your husbands (5:21–22). In a first-century context, to "submit" (*hypatassō*) is a word for order that was used to designate role relationships in various kinds of social structures. In contrast to the word "obey" (*hypakouō*), "submit" implies a voluntary yielding to one who has authority in a leadership structure. Submission is thus used in contexts where soldiers follow their commanders, members of the church yield to their leaders (see 1 Peter 3:5), and all people to the governing authorities of the state (see Rom. 13:1).

▶ **Josephus and Philo on Marriage**

First-century Jewish writers Josephus and Philo provide insight into some common Jewish attitudes about the wife's responsibility in marriage. Both stress blind obedience (versus submission) and say nothing of a husband's responsibility to love and serve his wife:

> For saith the Scripture, "A woman is inferior to her husband in all things" [in reality, there is no such verse any-

where in the Old Testament]. Let her, therefore, be obedient to him; not so that he should abuse her, but that she may acknowledge her duty to her husband; for God hath given the authority to the husband.[A-3]

Wives must be in servitude to their husbands, a servitude not imposed by violent treatment but promoting obedience in all things.[A-4]

▶ Aemilius Paulus and Papiria

The absence of the kind of love Paul describes as essential in marriage is well illustrated by the attitude of Aemelius Paulus toward his wife, as told by Florence Dupont:

> Aemilius Paullus had married Papiria, daughter of a former consul. Papiria was the perfect wife and gave her husband two sons, both of whom proved exceptional men.... Socially, Papiria was everything that was expected of her: she was beautiful, virtuous and fertile. Aemelius Paullus, however, decided to divorce her. "Why?" he was asked. "Is she not discreet? Is she not beautiful? Is she not fruitful?" Aemilius Paullus then held out his shoe, saying: "Is this not handsome? Is it not new? But not one of you can see where it pinches my foot." So he married another woman.[A-5]

In the first occurrence, Paul takes the dramatic step of enjoining a mutual submission. This flows out of the teaching of Jesus, who calls his disciples to serve one another and resist the temptation to "lord it over" each other (Mark 10:42–45). Elsewhere, Paul encourages believers to defer to the needs and interests of others by considering fellow believers even more highly than they consider themselves (Phil. 2:2–3). This involves subduing pride and self-oriented pursuits.

Nevertheless, Paul does not eliminate the social structuring of submission. He clearly maintains a role distinction between men and women in the marriage relationship and expects the man to assume a role of leadership. Yet Paul carefully qualifies the kind of leadership the husband is to provide.

The husband is the head of the wife as Christ is the head of the church (5:23). Paul has already used head-body imagery twice in this letter to describe the role of Christ in relationship to the church (see comments on 1:22–23 and 4:16). Here he applies the imagery to the role of the husband in the marriage relationship. Just as Christ provides leadership to the church and is its principal source of provision, the husband is called to the same function on behalf of his wife.

Husbands, love your wives, just as Christ loved the church and gave himself up for her (5:25). The kind of leadership the husband should exert is not defined by the prevailing cultural trends, but by the example of Christ himself. Above all the husband's leadership is governed by a self-sacrificial love. This admonition to the men flew in the face of many heavy-handed and demeaning attitudes of men toward their wives in antiquity—both in Judaism and in Greco-Roman culture (see "Josephus and Philo On Marriage" and "Aemelius Paulus and Papiria").

The washing with water (5:26). Paul is alluding here to the image of a marital covenant that Yahweh entered with Jerusalem. The Lord told his people, " 'I gave you my solemn oath and entered into a covenant with you', declares the Sovereign LORD, 'and you became mine. I bathed you with water and washed the blood from you ... you became very beautiful and rose to be a queen'" (Ezek. 16:8–13). The church is not cleansed by literal water (although there may be an allusion to baptism here); rather, the effective factor for salvation is the Word of God, the gospel, rooted in the blood of Christ that cleanses believers from all sin.

He feeds and cares for it (5:29). Both of these words appear in a papyrus marriage contract that delineates the husband's responsibilities for his wife: "to cherish and nourish and clothe her."[49]

This is a profound mystery (5:32). Paul is not referring to marriage as a deep mystery (and thus to marriage as a sacrament) or even mystery as it was used in the mystery religions of the area. The *mystery* he speaks of here is the intimate relationship of Christ to the church. This is consistent with his usage of this term throughout the letter (1:9; 3:3, 4, 9; 6:19), where it always speaks of something concealed that God has now revealed in Christ.

Children and Parents (6:1–4)

Children, obey your parents in the Lord (6:1). This command upholds the household authority structure common in the ancient world. In Jewish homes as well as Roman or Greek families, it was taken for granted that children should respond to their parents with total obedience. The distinctive contribution of this passage is that children are given an added incentive. The Lord himself expects children to have an attitude of obedience to parents. This is proper and essential for a Christian household.

Honor your father and mother (6:2). Paul now cites the fifth of the ten commandments to provide further support and perspective on children's obedience to their parents (Ex. 20:12; Deut. 5:16). Honoring and respecting parents was a social expectation that cut across all cultures in first-century society. In Gentile circles, honoring one's parents is regarded as important as honoring the gods. In Judaism, the fifth commandment is upheld by many writers, especially the wisdom literature. Note, for example, Sirach 3:8–11:

> *Honor your father by word and deed,*
> *that a blessing from him may come*
> *upon you. . . .*
> *Do not glorify yourself by dishonoring*
> *your father,*
> *for your father's dishonor is no*
> *glory to you.*
> *The glory of one's father is one's own*
> *glory,*
> *and it is a disgrace for children not*
> *to respect their mother.*

The first commandment with a promise (6:2). "Honor your father and mother" is the first of the Ten Commandments that treats human relationships (following the first four, which deal with one's relationship to God). It is also the only one of the ten that specifically has a promise attached to it.

Fathers, don't exasperate your children (6:4). In the exercise of authority and discipline, fathers are called to exercise sensitivity and moderation. This is consistent with the advice of some other ancient writers. The Greek writer Menander, for instance, says, "A father who is always threatening does not receive much reverence," and "One should correct a child by not hurting him but persuading him." Another writer cautions, "Do not be harsh with your children but be gentle."[50]

The training and instruction of the Lord (6:4). The ultimate responsibility for nurturing the children in the Christian faith lies with the father. He needs to pass on to them the apostolic tradition about Christ and his kingdom and help mold his children's lives into conformity with the will of God.

Slaves and Masters (6:5–9)

Slavery in the Roman world differed significantly from slavery in the New World. Yet slaves in antiquity were still considered possessions over which the owner had powerful rights. Centuries earlier, Aristotle could say, "A slave is a man's chattel" and "a living tool."[51] Given the fact that one-third or more of the population consisted of slaves, fifteen to twenty people in a house church of forty-five may have been slaves. In this passage, Paul assumes that slaves are full members of the church and share equally with their masters in all of the blessings of new life in Christ.

Obey your earthly masters (6:5). At this time and in this letter, Paul does not challenge the social order with respect to the institution of slavery, but gives perspective on how Christian slaves can live out their faith within this Roman social structure.

Like slaves of Christ (6:6). Paul clarifies that their allegiance and ownership does not lie ultimately with their human masters, but with Christ himself. They belong to him and are obligated to serve him.

Serve wholeheartedly (6:7). Some ancient writers spoke of "wholehearted service" or "enthusiasm" (*eunoia*) as a virtue for slaves.[52] One second-century A.D. papyrus even refers to a number of slaves who were set free because of their enthusiasm and affection in serving their master.[53]

Do not threaten them (6:9). Close to the same time that Paul was writing this letter, a Roman lawyer named Gaius Cassius Longinus addressed the Roman senate seeking retribution on the slaves of a former consul who was murdered by one of his slaves in his own home. Longinus cannot believe that the man's other slaves knew nothing of the plot or did anything to stop the murder. He pleads, "the only way to keep down this scum is

▶ Why There Wasn't a Massive Slave Revolt in the First Century

There is no evidence in ancient literature of a slave rebellion with the abolition of slavery as its goal. Why? Not only was Roman-era slavery a nonracial institution (there were slaves of all races), but most slaves could reasonably expect emancipation by the time they reached thirty years of age. Nor was the work of a slave limited to hard labor; slaves worked in a variety of different occupations—including household management, teaching, business, and industry—and many even owned property. Because of the poverty of many free laborers, the economic and living conditions of slaves were often far better. This led many free laborers to sell themselves into slavery as a means of economic advancement.[A-6] This is not to say that slavery was essentially an ungodly structure that deprived a person of freedom and dignity. It is simply to affirm that Roman era slavery did not share all of the same features of New World slavery that would ignite a rebellion.

▶The Story of the Ephesian Wrestler

An ancient writer named Pausanias relates an interesting and relevant parable about an Ephesian wrestler who traveled to Olympia, Greece, to compete in the games. The athlete was unbeateable in the wrestling event, winning match after match. During one of the competitions, however, the referee discovered he was wearing an anklet inscribed with the six Ephesian Grammata—the magical words invoking spiritual powers. This was immediately removed, whereupon his opponent from Miletus proceeded to three consecutive victories over him because of his loss of magical power.[A-7]

by intimidation."[54] Certainly not all Roman slave owners had this attitude or threatened their slaves. Jewish slave owners were in fact warned against undue severity.[55]

There is no favoritism with him (6:9). Paul reminds the wealthy slave owners that they will curry no special favor with God based on their social status. God is impartial and defers to no one according to social position. The Torah reveals that "the LORD your God is God of gods and Lord of lords, the great God, mighty and awesome, who shows no partiality" (Deut. 10:17).

Spiritual Warfare (6:10–20)

Paul says more about the struggle believers have with the evil supernatural realm here than anywhere else in his other letters. This may be due in large measure to the fact that most of these believers came to the Lord from a background in magic, astrology, witchcraft, goddess worship, and various mystery cults. Paul now prepares these believers for resisting the ongoing hostile work of the powers of darkness.

Be strong in the Lord (6:10). The emphasis of this command lies not with the verbal form of *dynamis* ("be strong"), but on "in the Lord." The people of this area are well aware of spiritual power, but they have been accustomed to receiving it from the wrong means—through helper spirits, incantations, rituals, formulas, and calling on their gods and goddesses. God desires to strengthen his people through a dynamic relationship to the Lord Jesus Christ.

Put on the full armor of God (6:11). Paul elaborates on his admonition to "be strong in the Lord" by using the imagery of the armor of God. The word that he uses for "full armor" (*panoplia*) never appears in the Old Testament, but it is used in Jewish wisdom literature.[56] Interpreters have often looked to the Roman soldier and his gear as the background for Paul's delineation of the six elements in the armor listed in 6:14–17. Yet each of the elements Paul lists is found in the Old Testament, especially in the book of Isaiah (see the chart).[57] It is also conspicuous that Paul does not mention weapons typically used by Roman soldiers, such as the heavy javelin (*pilum*) and greaves (leg armor).[58] It is important not to overinterpret the metaphors, but rather focus on the spiritual gifts and virtues associated with them.

So that you can take your stand (6:11). Forms of the verb "stand" appear four times in the next four verses. Paul stresses the fact that there is a supernatural being who is bent on promoting the demise of God's people.

Our struggle (6:12). Paul shifts the image from warfare to wrestling. Wrestling (*palē*) was a popular event in the games held in Ephesus, Smyrna, Pergamum, and all over Asia Minor. This image communicates more of the directness of the struggle.

Against the powers of this dark world (6:12). For his third expression in this list of powers (see comments on 1:21), Paul uses a word that appears nowhere else in the New Testament or the LXX—the term *kosmokratores* (lit. trans., "world powers"). The word does appear, however, in the Greek magical papyri (used

◀

ARMOR

Model reconstructions of a Roman breastplate and sword.

Spiritual Warfare Imagery		
Image	**Background**	**Spiritual Weapon**
1. Belt . . . buckled around your waist	Isa. 11:5	Truth
2. Breastplate	Isa. 59:17	Righteousness
3. Feet fitted	Isa. 52:7	Gospel of peace
4. Shield	(Isa. 21:5; Ps. 35:2) —23 times in the Old Testament	Faith
5. Helmet	Isa. 59:17	Salvation
6. Sword	(Isa. 49:2) —178 times in the Old Testament	Spirit/Word of God Prayer

of the gods Helios, Ra, Hermes, and Sarapis), some astrological texts (used of the planets), and a Roman inscription, where it refers to the gods Sarapis and Mithras.[59] The term is also used in a Jewish magical text, where it refers to the astral-demonic powers of the zodiac, who afflict people in a variety of ways.[60] The word is therefore known both to Gentile and Jewish readers. It is possible that Paul intends this word to be understood as his interpretation of the Ephesian Artemis and the other gods and goddesses worshiped in that city. Far from being beneficial or helpful deities, they should be regarded as evil spirits of "this dark world" (see also 1 Cor. 10:20).

When the day of evil comes (6:13). The Old Testament prophets anticipated a period of evil that they spoke of as "the day of disaster."[61] Apocalyptic Judaism spoke frequently of the evil character of the last days. Paul also speaks in these terms, but understands this time to be now. He speaks of "the present evil age" (Gal. 1:4) and encourages the Ephesians to redeem the time "because the days are evil" (Eph. 5:16). Although he still anticipates a time when Christ will return in judgment and wrath—"the day of the Lord," the present days are filled with evil and are a time of struggle and conflict

with the demonic.[62] The singular "day of evil" probably refers to particular periods within this time when demonic attack, manifestations of evil, and temptation are unusually strong.

With which you can extinguish all of the flaming arrows of the evil one (6:16). Flammable arrows were common and effective weapons in antiquity. They were used by Israelites and other Middle Easterners (see Ps. 7:13), Greeks, and Romans. The arrows typically had a clump of fiber attached near the point that had been dipped in pitch and set on fire. According to the Greek historian Thucydides (2.75.5), wooden shields were sometimes coated in leather and soaked in water before a battle so that they could not be ignited and could effectively subdue flaming arrows. The image of the devil hurling fiery arrows at God's servants is reminiscent of his angry opposition to the Seventy as they were

right ▶

ARMOR

An Ephesian monument of a soldier with a helmet, shield, boots, and a sword.

R E F L E C T I O N S

HOW DOES ONE PUT ON THE ARMOR OF GOD? THE corporate dimension of the passage and the way Paul reflects on the role of prayer—not only here, but also in Ephesians 1 and 3— suggest that a key part of spiritual warfare is in joining other Christians in praying for each other. Just as a soldier would need help in putting on his armor, we are called to arm each other through prayer. This passage sets an agenda for small group prayer times!

sent by Jesus on a mission. Jesus said, "I saw Satan fall like lightning from heaven" (Luke 10:18).

I am an ambassador in chains (6:20). Paul reminds the readers that he is bound as a prisoner in Rome.

Pray that I may declare it fearlessly (6:20). Twice at the end of this spiritual warfare passage Paul asks these dear believers to pray for God to make him bold in declaring the gospel. Although we are not accustomed to thinking of the apostle Paul as capable of intimidation, it appears that he may have some fear and a loss of nerve that he attributes to the work of the evil one through his circumstances in Rome. Paul does not hesitate to ask his fellow believers to intercede in prayer for him.

Personal Remarks and Closing (6:21–24)

Paul concludes his letter in the most personal of touches. He indicates that he will send his trusted colleague Tychicus to fill the Ephesians in on his circumstances. He draws his letter to an end by prayerfully wishing for them a manifestation of God's peace, love, and grace.

Tychicus (6:21). Tychicus is one of Paul's missionary colleagues with him in Rome as he writes this letter. According to Acts, Tychicus was from the province of Asia, which may very well mean that he was actually from Ephesus.[63] He is not mentioned in the account of Paul's ministry in Ephesus (Acts 19) nor did he accompany Paul on his harrowing sea voyage to Rome. This means he probably journeyed from Ephesus to Rome specifically to help Paul. Paul's warm description of him as "a dear brother and faithful servant in the Lord" indicates that the Lord has used him to encourage Paul in his difficult circumstances. Now out of his concern for the Asia Minor Christians, Paul sends Tychicus back home to Asia Minor, where he will deliver the letter to the Colossians (see Col. 4:7) and this letter to the Ephesians.

ANNOTATED BIBLIOGRAPHY

Arnold, Clinton E. *Power and Magic: The Concept of Power in Ephesians.* Grand Rapids: Baker, 1997 (formerly titled *Ephesians: Power and Magic*; originally published as SNTSMS 63; Cambridge: Cambridge Univ. Press, 1989).

This is a detailed background study of Ephesians focusing on the theme of power and spirit powers. The book highlights and explains the relevance of the local occultism, magical practices, astrology, and the cult of the Ephesian Artemis (Diana) for explaining the emphasis on the power of God and spiritual warfare in Ephesians.

Bruce, F. F. *The Epistles to the Colossians, to Philemon, and to the Ephesians.* NICNT. Grand Rapids: Eerdmans, 1984.

As always, Bruce provides helpful commentary on each passage with useful historical background information.

Lincoln, Andrew T. *Ephesians.* WBC 42. Dallas: Word, 1990.

This five-hundred-page volume is one of the best detailed commentaries available on Ephesians. There are abun-dant historical and cultural insights scattered throughout this commentary.

Moritz, Thorsten. *A Profound Mystery: The Use of the Old Testament in Ephesians.* NovTSup 85. Leiden: Brill, 1996.

An outstanding study of the use of the Old Testament throughout Ephesians.

O'Brien, Peter T. *Ephesians.* PNTC. Grand Rapids: Eerdmans, 1999.

This is the best all-around commentary on Ephesians.

Snodgrass, Klyne. *Ephesians.* NIVAC. Grand Rapids: Zondervan, 1996.

Snodgrass does an excellent job of interpreting Ephesians and discerning the implications of the text for contemporary life.

Stott, John R. W. *The Message of Ephesians.* The Bible Speaks Today. Downers Grove: InterVarsity, 1979.

In finding a commentary on Ephesians that combines exegetical insight with good application, it is hard to beat the work of John Stott.

CHAPTER NOTES

Main Text Notes
1. Strabo 14.1.24.
2. Josephus, *Ant.* 14.10.11–12 §§223–27; 14.10.25 §§262–64.
3. See Richard E. Oster, "Ephesus As a Religious Center Under the Principate, I. Paganism Before Constantine," *ANRW* 2.18.3 (1990): 1661–726.
4. See James Walters, "Egyptian Religions in Ephesus," in *Ephesos: Metropolis of Asia* (HTS 41; Valley Forge, Pa.: Trinity Press International, 1995): 281–309.
5. Antipater, *Anthologia Graeca* 9.58.
6. See C. E. Arnold, "Magic," *DPL*, 580–83; idem, "Magic and Astrology," *DLNT*, 701–5.
7. See "Adoption," *OCD³*, s.v.
8. See Dan. 2:18, 19, 27–30, 47.
9. See Dan. 2:28, 29, 45.
10. See R. Schippers, "Seal," *NIDNTT*, 3:497.
11. Herodotus 2.113; *3 Macc.* 2:29–30.
12. 1QS 2:3.
13. See *1 En.* 6:7–8; 61:10; *2 En.* 20:1; *T. Levi* 3:8; *T. Sol.* 3:6; 20:15; *3 Bar.* 12:3; *T. Ab.* 13:10 (shorter recension).
14. *PGM* 61.2; CI.52; 7:580–90.
15. See Dan. 2:44; 7:14, 18, 27.
16. Cf. Ezek. 44:4; also Isa. 6:1; Hag. 2:7.
17. Dan. 10:13, 20–21; 12:1.
18. Matt. 9:34; 12:24; Mark 3:22; Luke 11:15; John 12:31; 14:30; 16:11.
19. *PGM* CI.39.
20. *T. Benj.* 3:4.
21. The best explanation of this can be found in W. D. Davies, *Paul and Rabbinic Judaism. Some Rabbinic Elements in Pauline Theology* (3d ed.; London: SPCK, 1970 [originally published in 1948]), ch. 2: "The Old Enemy: The Flesh and Sin," 17–35.
22. See Deut. 5:10; 7:9, 12; Ps. 89:28.
23. *T. Ab.* 13:1–14. See also *4 Ezra* 9:7 and 13:23.
24. *m. ʾAbot* 2:8 (Danby, 448).

25. Gen. 15:7–21; 17:1–21; 26:2–5; 28:13–15; Ex. 24:1–8; 2 Sam. 7.

26. Josephus, *J.W.* 5.5.2 §§193–94; 6.2.4 §§124–26; *Ant.* 15.11.5 §417.

27. One complete tablet written in Greek is on display in the Archaeological Museum in Istanbul, Turkey. Half of another is housed in the Rockefeller Museum in Jerusalem.

28. An English translation is given and discussed in Barrett, *Background*, 53 (no. 50). See also the discussions in Douglas R. Edwards, "-Gentiles, Court of the," *ABD* 2.963; Schürer, *History*, 2.222.

29. See "Temple Foundation Stone Discovered," *Christianity Today* 36 (May 18, 1992): 52.

30. Josephus, *Ant.* 15.11.1 §380; 20.9.7 §§219–23.

31. 1 Cor. 2:6–8; cf. Luke 22:3; John 13:27.

32. Mark 2:40; see also Matt. 9:18; 15:25.

33. See *PGM* 4.964–74, 979–85.

34. For the Aramaic text and translation as well as an in-depth discussion, see W. Hall Harris III, *The Descent of Christ. Ephesians 4:7–11 and Traditional Hebrew Imagery* (AGJU 32; Leiden: Brill, 1996), 65, 97.

35. For further details, see Clinton E. Arnold, "Jesus Christ: 'Head' of the Church," in *Jesus of Nazareth: Lord and Christ. Essays on the Historical Jesus and New Testament Christology*, eds. M. M. B. Turner and J. B. Green (Grand Rapids: Eerdmans, 1994), 346–66.

36. James 1:19–20; see also Prov. 15:1, 18; 22:24; 29:11; Eccl. 7:9.

37. Translation from G. Vermes, *The Complete Dead Sea Scrolls in English* (New York: Penguin Press, 1997), 132.

38. Plutarch, *Moralia* 488c (as cited in Lincoln, *Ephesians*, 302).

39. *T. Dan* 4:7.

40. *m. ʿAbod. Zar.* 2.1.

41. See, e.g., *T. Reu.* 1.6; 2.1; 3.3; 4.6; 5.1, 3; 6.1; *T. Sim.* 5.3; *T. Iss.* 7.2.

42. *T. Jud.* 19:1.

43. *T. Reu.* 4:6.

44. Philo, *Spec. Laws* 1.23.

45. See R. P. Martin, "Hymns, Hymn Fragments, Songs, Spiritual Songs," *DPL*, 419–23.

46. See Albert Heinrichs, "Dionysus," *OCD*, 479–82; Walter Burkert, *Ancient Mystery Cults* (Cambridge, Mass.: Harvard Univ. Press, 1987), 109–11.

47. Isa. 32:15; 44:3; Ezek. 36:25–27; 39:28–29; Joel 2:28–29.

48. See Ramsay MacMullen, *Paganism in the Roman Empire* (New Haven, Conn.: Yale Univ. Press, 1981), 15–18.

49. The text is quoted in Best, *Ephesians*, 550.

50. Cited in Lincoln, *Ephesians*, 406 (Menander as quoted in Stobaeus, *Anthologia* 4.26.7, 13; Ps.-Phocylides 207).

51. Aristotle, *Eth. Nic.* 5.1134b, 8.1161b.

52. See the texts cited in Lincoln, *Ephesians*, 422.

53. P.Oxy. 494.6.

54. Tacitus, *Ann.* 14.44

55. Sir. 4:30; 7:20; 33:31.

56. See Wisd. Sol. 5:17–20.

57. See Thorsten Moritz, *A Profound Mystery. The Use of the Old Testament in Ephesians* (NovTSup 85; Leiden: Brill, 1996), 178–212.

58. See Jonathan C. N. Coulston, "Arms and Armour (Roman)," in *OCD*[3], 174.

59. See Arnold, *Power and Magic*, 65–68.

60. *T. Sol.* 8:2; 18:2.

61. Jer. 17:17–18; Obad. 13.

62. 1 Cor. 1:8; 5:5; 1 Thess. 5:2.

63. The Western text of Acts (codex D) specifically adds that he was an Ephesian.

Sidebar and Chart Notes

A-1. From Manilius 1.25–112, as cited in Georg Luck, *Arcana Mundi* (Baltimore: John's Hopkins Univ. Press, 1985), 325.

A-2. Plutarch, *Quaest. conv.* 7.5.

A-3. Josephus, *Ag. Ap.* 2.25 §201.

A-4. Philo, *Hypothetica* 7.3.

A-5. Florence Dupont, *Daily Life in Ancient Rome* (Oxford: Blackwell, 1989), 114. The original source is Plutarch, *Aemilius Paullus* 5.

A-6. On slavery in the Roman world, see S. Scott Bartchy, "Slavery," in *ABD*, 6:65–73 and his book, *MALLON CHRESAI: First Century Slavery and the Interpretation of 1 Cor 7:21* (SBLDS 11; Missoula, Mont., 1973 [repr. 1985]).

A-7. Pausanias as cited in Eustathius, *Comm. ad Hom.* 19.247. The account is also cited in The Suda.

PHILIPPIANS

by Frank Thielman

First Century Philippi

In Paul's time Philippi was an important city in the Roman province of Macedonia. It was located on a fertile plain in the highlands about ten miles northwest of the port city Neapolis (modern Kavalla in northern Greece), and the Via Egnatia—the primary road linking Italy with Asia—ran through the city. After the Romans conquered Macedonia at the Battle of Pydna in 167 B.C. they divided it into four districts.[1] Philippi was located in the first of these districts and probably contended with Amphipolis (the district's capital) and Thessalonica for the coveted title of "leading city" of its region.[2]

Mark Anthony and Octavian designated Philippi a Roman colony and enlarged its territory after their defeat of Brutus and Cassius in a famous battle fought on the plains and hills surrounding the city in 42 B.C.[3] From that time the city and its surrounding regions became a favorite location for settling Roman soldiers whose term of service in the

PHILIPPI

▶ **Philippians**
IMPORTANT FACTS:

- **AUTHOR:** Paul (with Timothy).
- **DATE:** A.D. 53 (if from Ephesus), or A.D. 62 (if from Rome).
- **OCCASION:**
  - To thank the Philippians for a gift.
  - To commend Epaphroditus for completing his assigned task.
  - To warn the Philippians against theological error.
  - To encourage the Philippians to strive for unity.
- **KEY THEMES:**
  1. The progress of the gospel as the basis for joy despite suffering.
  2. Attaining Christian unity by following the selfless example of Christ.
  3. A right standing with God available by faith in Christ alone.
  4. Mature faith as working faith.

army had ended.[4] As a result, by Paul's time, Philippi had a decidedly Roman character. In first-century inscriptions found at the site of Philippi, Latin is the dominant tongue. Some of these inscriptions mention duumviri, aediles, and quaestors, all Roman terms for city officials—and clear evidence that in Paul's time the city was administered according to Roman custom. Moreover, the architectural remains of buildings and monuments from the first century are reminiscent of Rome: a Roman forum, Roman baths, and an arch marking the limit of the city's sacred, uncultivated area (*pomerium*).[5]

PHILIPPI

▼

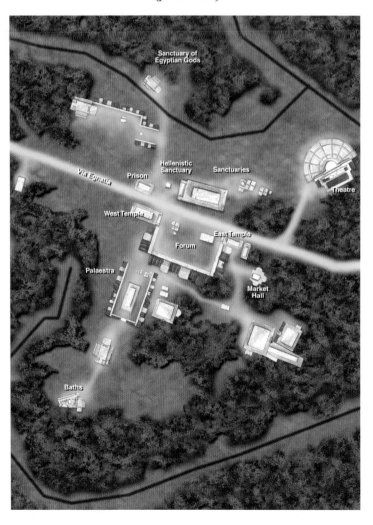

Important commercial centers, with their wide variety of influences, teemed with religious activity, and Philippi was no exception. Inscriptions from around Paul's time show the presence of a sanctuary dedicated to Dionysius (Bacchus) and other deities associated with him: Liber, Libera, and Hercules.[6] Themes of fertility often accompanied worship of Dionysius, and the Dionysian mystery cult seems to have given him a role in assuring a happy life for the dead. Women played an especially prominent role in the worship of Dionysius and his associates in Philippi.[7] Nearly eighty depictions of the goddess Diana appear in reliefs carved into the hill above Philippi, and although they come from a period after Paul, they probably reflect religious convictions current during his time. Diana was associated with fertility, childbirth, and children, typical concerns of ancient women. Most of her followers, both priestesses and devotees, seem to have been women.[8] The Thracian Horseman also appears in seven hillside reliefs. He was especially connected with the safe conduct of the soul into the afterlife.[9] In addition, archaeologists have turned up an altar dedicated to the emperor Augustus and a sanctuary dedicated to the worship of some 140 Egyptian deities.[10]

The Gospel Comes to Philippi

Into this cacophony of religious activity, Paul and his friends Silas, Timothy, and Luke brought the gospel. Taking the gospel to Philippi had not been Paul's idea. After traveling through central Asia Minor, Paul, Silas, and Timothy had wanted to continue north to Bithynia, but "the Spirit of Jesus would not allow them to" (Acts 16:7), and they had been forced to turn east toward Troas. There Paul had a vision of a man from Macedonia, who begged him to "come . . . and help us" (16:9), and Paul and his friends, now accompanied by Luke, obediently went (16:10–12). Their ship from Troas landed at Neapolis, and from there they followed the Via Egnatia to Philippi.

Paul discovered no synagogue in the city, but only a place of prayer where a few women gathered to call on the name of the God of Abraham, Isaac, and Jacob. Luke tells us that this place was "outside the city gate" (Acts 16:13). Could this mean that their gathering place lay outside the sacred precincts of the Roman *pomerium*, marked by a marble arch?[11] Paul explained the gospel to the group of women gathered there, and a woman named Lydia, together with her household, believed. She must have been wealthy, for not only was she a businesswoman, but she owned a house large enough to accommodate Paul and his companions during their visit to Philippi (16:14–15).

Before long, however, storm clouds gathered over Paul's ministry in the city: The apostle angered the owners of a slave girl by exorcising her of a demon that enabled her to earn "a great deal of money for her owners" by telling fortunes (Acts 16:16–19). The enraged slaveholders dragged Paul and Silas before the city magistrates and charged them with being Jews and creating a stir by advocating "customs unlawful for us Romans to accept or practice" (16:20–21). At the

THE
MEDITERRANEAN
WORLD
▼

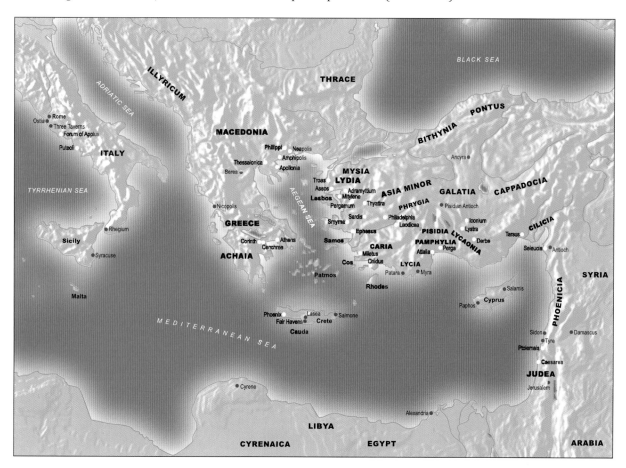

magistrates' orders, Paul and Silas were stripped, beaten, and thrown into prison (16:22). Despite the conversion of the jailer (16:31–34) and an apology to Paul from the magistrates for failing to give Roman citizens a proper trial (16:35–37), the persecution of the fledgling Philippian church continued (Phil. 1:27–30).

The Reasons for Paul's Letter

EGNATIAN WAY

A portion of the pavement of the *Via Egnatia,* the principal Roman road that traversed Macedonia from Byzantium to Dyrrhachium.
▼

We do not know exactly where Paul was when he wrote Philippians. He was in a city large enough to have a *praetorium* or official government headquarters (Phil. 1:13, NIV, "palace guard"), but whether this was Rome, Ephesus, or Caesarea has been a matter for scholarly debate over the years. Whatever the city, however, Paul was in prison when he wrote (1:7,

13–14, 17), and he wrote in part to thank the Philippians for gifts that they had sent to him through their messenger Epaphroditus: "I am amply supplied," he says, "now that I have received from Epaphroditus the gifts you sent" (4:18; cf. 1:5; 2:25; 4:10, 14).

The Philippians' gifts and Paul's need to thank them provided a context in which to address four other concerns.

1. Paul intended to send Epaphroditus back to the Philippians earlier than they expected because he had become ill and the Philippians had become worried about him. In doing so, Paul wanted the Philippians to know that Epaphroditus had not failed in his duty, but instead deserved rich commendation, "because he almost died for the work of Christ" (2:30).

2. Paul had left a persecuted community behind after his initial visit. That persecution had continued unabated, and Paul, since he was in prison himself, wanted to provide an example to the Philippians of how a believer should respond to physical suffering and social ostracisim for the faith. He tells them, "You are going through the same struggle you saw I had, and now hear that I still have" (1:30; cf. 2:17–18; 3:17). Paul's example shows that the believer's joy should be tied to the progress of the gospel, not to physical comfort or social acceptance (1:18).

3. Paul wanted to warn the Philippians against two errors that he has seen tear apart other churches under his care: thinking that the boundaries of Christianity are defined by the Mosaic law (cf. Galatians) and that Christians who have "arrived" spiritually can do anything they like with their bodies (cf. 1 Corinthians). If the letter was written from Ephesus, the wounds created by these problems

were fresh, and Paul warned the Philippians against them in 3:1–4:1. Christianity is a matter of faith in Christ, Paul says (3:1–11), and mature Christians know that they must never rest on their laurels (3:12–4:1).

4. Paul had apparently learned from Epaphroditus that the Philippians were quarreling with one another. Paul is concerned that this may lead to a tarnished witness to the outside world where the Philippian Christians "shine like stars in the universe" (2:15; cf. 1:27; 2:1–11, 14; 4:2). In light of this, he urged the Philippians to have the mind of Christ, who in obedience to God and in service to others, humbled himself and suffered death on the cross (2:1–11).

Introduction (1:1–2)

Ancient letters typically began with the name of the sender, followed by the name of the recipient and the common salutation *charein* ("Greetings!"). Paul changes *charein* to *charis*, the Greek word for "grace," and adds the typical Jewish greeting, "peace." Such changes in the opening lines of letters were as rare in ancient times as they are today, but they were not wholly unknown. The ancient moral philosopher Epicurus (341–270 B.C.) apparently modified the openings of his letters so that they reflected his belief that pleasure was the highest of life's ideals. "Live well," he sometimes wrote in the salutation.[12] Nothing was more important to Paul, however, than the "grace of our Lord Jesus Christ" (2 Cor. 8:9) and the "peace with God" effected by that grace (Rom. 3:24–25; 5:1). Accordingly, the salutations in all thirteen of Paul's letters refer to "grace" and "peace."

Paul and Timothy (1:1). Paul couples his name with Timothy's name in this letter as he does at the beginning of five other letters (2 Corinthians, Colossians, 1 Thessalonians, 2 Thessalonians, and Philemon). Despite this, Paul alone composed the letter, as his frequent use of "I" and his

◀

PHILIPPI

Remains of the forum and agora.

commendation of Timothy in 2:20–22 show. Why then mention Timothy at all? Perhaps Timothy served as Paul's secretary, recording the letter as Paul dictated it. *Amanuenses,* as they were called in Greek, were commonly used to compose letters at the dictation of others. In addition, Paul probably wanted the Philippians to know that his most trusted coworker ("I have no one else like him," 2:20) and their friend ("you know that Timothy has proved himself," 2:22) joined him in the expression of friendship represented by the letter and in the admonitions that Paul wanted the Philippians to hear (see "Timothy Among Paul's Coworkers," below).

Servants of Christ Jesus (1:1). The term "servants" might give the impression that Paul's metaphor refers to hired household help. Paul calls himself and Timothy not "servants" in this sense, however, but "slaves" of Christ Jesus. Like every major urban center in the Roman empire, Philippi would have had a large slave population, and the Philippians would

have inevitably heard in the term "slaves" overtones of humility and submission. Is Paul modeling here the attitude of humble service that he encourages the Philippians to adopt toward one another in 2:3–4?

Overseers (1:1). Two hundred miles to the southeast of Philippi, at the southern end of the Aegean Sea, was the island of Rhodes. Here the term "overseers" was used on an inscription from the second or first century B.C. of the five community officials that formed a kind of town council. Another inscription from the island also refers to an official in the temple of Apollo as an "overseer."[13] As religious communities, it is natural that the churches Paul founded in Ephesus (Acts 20:28; 1 Tim. 3:2) and on Crete (Titus 1:7) had an analogous office of "overseer." These officials were to tend carefully the churches over whom God had placed them as stewards (1 Tim. 3:2; Titus 1:7). As part of this task, they were to take special care to keep false teachers at bay (Acts 20:28; cf. Phil. 3:1–11).

Deacons (1:1). In the city of Magnesia, an ancient Greek inscription includes a "cook" and a "deacon" among local temple officials.[14] In early Christianity too churches served meals and chose certain people from within the church to wait tables (*diakoneō;* Acts 6:1–2). The duties of these helpers must have quickly broadened to include a variety of charitable and administrative tasks—responsibilities that required deacons to be people of unblemished character (1 Tim. 3:8–13). Unlike the deacons in pagan religions, Christian deacons would have patterned their service after that of Jesus who "did not come to be served [aor. pass. inf. of *diakoneō*], but to

serve [aor. act. inf. of *diakoneō*], and to give his life as a ransom for many" (Mark 10:45).[15]

Thanksgiving Prayer (1:3–8)

Paul typically follows the introductions to his letters with a section in which he tells the congregation to whom he is writing why he thanks God for them. These thanksgivings briefly mention themes that Paul will develop in the course of the letter. If the Philippians had received other letters from Paul (3:1), they may have understood this characteristic of his letters and may have known to listen carefully for the letter's leading themes as Epaphroditus read the thanksgiving to them.

Your partnership from the first day until now (1:5). When Paul speaks of partnership, he is speaking of the practical hospitality and material help that the Philippians had given to him ever since he first met them. The first Philippian convert, Lydia, had invited Paul and his companions to stay at her house during their visit to the city (Acts 16:15). When Paul left Philippi and pressed westward along the Egnatian Way to Thessalonica, the Philippians more than once sent him gifts to help him in his work (Phil. 4:16). Even after he left the province of Macedonia, they and they alone continued to help him in practical ways (4:15). Although poor, they contributed generously to the collection for the saints in Jerusalem (2 Cor. 8:1–5), and they had most recently sent Paul both money and the companionship of Epaphroditus (2:25; 4:18). It is no wonder that as some Christians where Paul was imprisoned sought his harm (1:17), he longed for this beloved congregation (1:8; 4:1).

The day of Christ Jesus (1:6, 10). Some of the Philippian Christians, such as Lydia, were familiar with Judaism (Acts 16:13–14) and would have probably readily understood the Old Testament background of this phrase. For others, Paul would have explained the ideas necessary for understanding it when he first preached among the Philippians. "Christ" in Greek means "anointed one" and refers to the anointed descendant of David—the Messiah—who would sit on David's throne forever, purge God's people of wickedness, and rule justly (Isa. 9:7; Jer. 23:5–6; see "God's Righteousness in Paul's Bible," below).[16] The gospel that Paul preached in Philippi proclaimed that the Messiah was Jesus of Nazareth and that although he had been crucified, God had raised him from the dead. He was still present with his people by his Spirit (1:19) and was at work among them to make them pure and blameless for the day when he would come again (1:10).

Defending and confirming the gospel (1:7). "Defending" is a technical term for mounting a defense in court against legal accusations. "Confirming" is also a technical legal term; it refers to a legal guarantee that, for example, a piece of property to be sold has no liens against it.[17] Paul's own legal situation, as he waited in prison for trial, may have suggested this imagery to him.

Intercessory Prayer (1:9–11)

Ancient letters between friends, family members, and business associates frequently included a brief statement that the person sending the letter prayed for the prosperity and health of the recipient. In a letter from the second century A.D. a young soldier named Theonas writes home to his mother Tetheus and after the letter's introduction says, "Before all else I pray that you are well; I myself am well and make obeisance on your behalf to the gods here."[18] Another letter from a military veteran named Papirius Apollinarius to an apparent business associate greets the recipient and then assures him that Papirius bows daily on his behalf "before the lord Serapis."[19] Paul prays to the God of Abraham, Isaac, Jacob, and Christ Jesus, and, unlike prayer after prayer in ancient pagan correspondence, he prays not for the material prosperity of the Philippians or even for their physical health, but that they might know God and live in ways that please him.

Pure and blameless (1:10). Paul prays that the Philippians might have knowledge and insight, enabling them to choose what is best from the various moral options that confront them. If they do this consistently, they will be "pure" and "blameless" on the day when the Messiah returns. The term "pure" means "unmixed" and could be used in the Attic period to refer to ethnic purity. Plato, for example, speaks of being "purely Greek and without barbarian mixture."[20] Paul uses the word in a figurative way typical of the Koine period to mean "unmixed with evil."[21] The word "blameless" means similarly doing no injustice or evil, and is a quality that pious Jews of the period could use of God. It was a divine quality, said one third-century B.C. Jew, that Gentiles should seek to imitate.[22]

Paul's Circumstances (1:12–18a)

Now I want you to know (1:12). In ancient letters to friends and family a phrase similar to this sometimes marked the beginning of a section of the letter that would give the recipients the latest news of their loved one. Young soldiers separated from their families by many miles frequently wrote such letters. Theonas, for example, wrote to his mother from his military camp to let her know that he was not seriously ill, as she had mistakenly heard, but was doing well. After the standard greetings, he says, "I want you to know that the reason I have not sent you a letter for such a long time is because I am in camp and not on account of illness; so do not worry yourself about me."[23] Paul begins the section of Philippians that gives news about his own circumstances (1:12–26) in the same way. Significantly, however, this section of the letter tells more about the progress of the gospel in the midst of Paul's circumstances than about the details of his health, the conditions of his imprisonment, or his strategy for defending himself at trial. Paul's life was so wrapped up with Christ and the gospel that to give news about himself was always to say how God was at work in Paul's circumstances to advance the gospel.

What has happened to me has really served to advance the gospel (1:12). The

moral philosopher Epicurus believed that when tragedy struck, he could still be happy if he turned his mind away from his unpleasant circumstances and concentrated on pleasurable thoughts. He put this principle into action during his final illness when, in the midst of excruciating pain, he wrote letters to his disciples Idomeneus and Hermarchus. Here he tells these two followers that he is turning his thoughts away from the pain of his circumstances to the pleasure of the philosophical discussions that they all had enjoyed in more pleasant times.[24] Later in Philippians, Paul will advocate that the Philippian Christians turn from the worries of their own persecutions to the contemplation not of pleasure but of the virtues: whatever is true, noble, right, pure, lovely, admirable, excellent, and praiseworthy (4:4–8).[25] He will also tell them that they should look to him as an example to follow in doing this (4:9). In 1:12–18a he provides that example. Here Paul mentally turns aside from his imprisonment and from his enemies to concentrate on God's advancement of the gospel through these difficult circumstances.[26] Like Epicurus, Paul is mentally turning away from pain to pleasure, but Paul found pleasure in the advancement of the gospel and the glory of God (1:11–12).

The whole palace guard (1:13). The phrase "palace guard" translates the Latin loanword *praetorium*, which literally means "military headquarters." Paul gives the word a figurative meaning: "the people who work in the *praetorium*." If he wrote from Rome, he probably meant "the praetorian [or palace] guard." If he wrote from Ephesus, he meant the staff who worked in the governor's headquarters, where he was imprisoned. News of

the advancement of the gospel among the praetorians in Rome would have been especially welcome to the Philippians. Since during Paul's time the praetorians were required to come either from Italy itself or from Rome's most sympathetic colonies, some of them may have come from Philippi. The Philippian Christians knew about them and, in the midst of their own experience of persecution, must have been cheered by the news that the gospel had even advanced to this elite enclave of the Roman world.

In chains for Christ (1:13). Roman custody was of four basic types: imprisonment (with or without chains), military custody (which might include being chained to a soldier), release into the custody of a trustworthy person, and release on one's own recognizance. Paul may have been under military guard, possibly chained to a soldier. This must have been an extraordinarily uncomfortable situation, since Paul would have to ask permission from the soldier guarding him to make any significant physical movement. The Christian bishop Ignatius shows just how unfriendly such guards could be. In a letter written in the early second century while on his way from Syrian Antioch to Rome for execution, Ignatius says that he is chained night and day to "wild beasts...[who] become worse when treated well."[27]

Put here for the defense of the gospel (1:16). Exactly why some who preached Christ in the city of Paul's imprisonment opposed the apostle and tried to make his affliction worse remains a mystery. When Paul says that his supporters know that he is in prison "for the defense of the gospel" (1:16), he may provide a clue to the reasoning of his opponents. Ancient Roman society placed immense value on public honor, and therefore imprison-

ment was profoundly shameful. Thus, when people of honor were led to prison, they sometimes tried to cover or hide their faces and were forced to lift or expose them in order to intensify their shame.[28] It is possible that Paul's rivals considered his imprisonment shameful and an embarrassment to the gospel (cf. 2 Tim. 1:16–17). His supporters knew, however, that Paul had no reason to be ashamed—he had been imprisoned because of his faithfulness in defending the gospel.

Selfish ambition (1:17). Prior to the New Testament, the only known use of this term is in Aristotle's *Politics* (5.3), where the philosopher used it to describe a greedy grasp for public office through unjust means.[29] Paul seems to use the expression in a similar way here to say that his opponents are not preaching Christ in order to promote the cause of the gospel, but are unfairly using Paul's imprisonment as a means of promoting their own agenda.

Paul Reflects on His Future (1:18b–26)

Will turn out for my deliverance . . . and . . . that I will in no way be ashamed (1:19–20). Although Paul nowhere indicates that he is quoting Scripture when

---

R E F L E C T I O N S

CHRISTIANS IN EVERY GENERATION HAVE HAD TO take courageous stands for the gospel against the prevailing winds of the societies in which they have lived. In the last generation the Confessing Church in Germany stood against the so-called "German Christians" who had sold out to the evil policies of the Third Reich. Where will the church of the twenty-first century be tempted to swim with the tide of society when the church ought to stand against it?

▶ The Praetorians

The "palace guard" or "praetorians" were the bodyguards of the Roman emperor. Whether Paul wrote Philippians from Ephesus during the reign of Claudius or from Rome during the reign of Nero, the praetorians would have consisted of twelve cohorts, possibly of 1,000 soldiers each.[A-1] The praetorians were extremely powerful. Only a few years prior to Paul's imprisonment among them they had succeeded in having Claudius proclaimed emperor after the assassination of Caligula in A.D. 41. Their purpose was to retain their position of power rather than relinquish it to the Roman senate and a republican form of government.[A-2]

he uses this phrase, it is a word-for-word citation of the Greek version of Job 13:16. Job says that he knows, contrary to his accusers, that his own iniquity is not the cause of his suffering. He uses the metaphor of standing trial before God and says that he is confident that after God has cross-examined him he will be saved. Similarly, Paul knows that whatever the outcome of his trial, when he stands before God he will have no cause for shame but will experience "salvation" (NIV, "deliverance").

Whether by life or by death . . . what shall I choose . . . I am torn between the two (1:20–23). The Philippian Christians lived within a culture that was deeply concerned with death and the meticulous care of the deceased. Paul's approach to death and life in 1:20–23 must have seemed extraordinarily casual to those in the Philippian church who were accustomed to such practices. Physical death was of little importance to him—living meant Christ, and because to die involved going to be with Christ eternally, this too was a gain.

Your progress (1:26). In 1:12 Paul spoke of the "advancement" (*prokopē*) of the gospel through his own circumstances. Now he uses the same word, translated "progress" in the NIV, to anticipate the discussion in the rest of the letters of the gospel's "advancement" among the Philippians. This is a rare word, used in the New Testament only in these two places and in 1 Timothy 4:15. By using it in this way, Paul is marking off the major divisions of his letter for those who will hear it read aloud. The ancients called this rhetorical device *inclusio*.

The Philippians' Circumstances (1:27–2:18)

Conduct yourselves (1:27). This phrase translates a single Greek verb (*politeueomai*) that appears only here and in Acts 23:1 in the New Testament. In both places it refers to one's conduct as a citizen. The Philippians were conscious of their privileged status as a Roman colony, one of only five cities in Macedonia granted the *ius Italicum*—the right to be governed by Roman law and to be

exempt from direct taxation.[30] The Philippian Christians must have stuck out like a sore thumb in this society. They were not willing to participate in the popular cult of the Roman emperor, nor were they willing to conduct the traditional funerary rites at the graves of their ancestors (see "Rock Reliefs and the Afterlife in Ancient Philippi," below). Neither step would have endeared them to government officials or to unbelieving family members. Both groups would have viewed them as bad citizens, a cause for shame to both city and family. With this admonition to live as citizens who are worthy of the Christian gospel, Paul is telling the Philippians that they are citizens of another, heavenly country (cf. 3:20) and should take their sense of shame and honor from it rather than from Philippi.

Contending (1:27). Here and in verse 30, where Paul speaks of his past and present "struggle," he uses athletic imagery to describe the conduct of Christians in the face of opposition. Around the time of Paul, the author of *4 Maccabees* used this imagery in a similar way to describe the "contest" that Jewish martyrs faced under the wicked Seleucid King Antiochus IV.[31] Like the labor of athletes, the struggle of persecuted Jews and Christians was often both physical and public. The persecuted people of God, however, engaged in this struggle for different reasons from their counterparts in the athletic arena. "They do it," Paul says in another place, "to get a crown that will not last; but we do it to get a crown that will last forever" (1 Cor. 9:25).

Encouragement . . . comfort . . . fellowship . . . tenderness . . . compassion (2:1). Like many people today, people in the Greco-Roman world often lived in anxiety about the future. Would they be victims of disease, famine, war, and an untimely death, or would Fate deal them a better hand? The ancients used magic to try to control the powers that they believed decided their future. But (they must have worried) would their incantations, sacrifices, and amulets work? Into all this the gospel brought the "encouragement" and "comfort" that a loving God created and controlled the world. It brought the good news that this God had shown his love through Jesus Christ, who in "tenderness" and "compassion" healed the sick and raised the dead in anticipation of a day when disease and death would disappear. The preaching of the gospel also established a "fellowship" of

▶ Rock Reliefs and the Afterlife in Ancient Philippi

On the hill that towers above Philippi ancient Philippians often carved into the living rock reliefs of goddesses and gods who would help them in the afterlife. Nine reliefs of the Greek goddess Diana show her in close proximity to a lunar crescent, a symbol of death and the afterlife. The hill also features carvings of the Thracian Horseman, who was thought to lead the deceased to heaven after death. Gravestones from the vicinity of Philippi also depict the Thracian Horseman and tell survivors of the deceased to visit the grave each year to conduct special ceremonies for the dead. Some devotees of the Horseman gathered in funerary associations whose task was to keep watch over the graves of deceased members. Although these reliefs and inscriptions come from about a century after Paul, the cults that produced them would have been thriving during the period of Paul's ministry.[A-3]

▶ Is 2:6–11 an Early Christian Hymn?

The early Christians sang not only the Psalter but "hymns and spiritual songs" also (Eph. 5:19; Col. 3:16). Paul may quote such songs in Colossians 1:15–20 and 1 Timothy 3:16. In the late nineteenth century, a few scholars began suggesting that Philippians 2:6–11 was also a hymn about the humiliation and exaltation of Christ, and during the twentieth century a number of detailed studies seemed to confirm this notion.[A-4] Like the other two passages, these verses begin with the pronoun "who," possibly a clue that they are an excerpt from a larger composition. They also use several words that appear nowhere else in Paul's letters, and they seem to fall naturally into two balanced parts, verses 6–8 describing Christ's humiliation and verses 9–11 his exaltation.

Other scholars, however, continue to maintain that these verses reflect a moment of impressive rhetoric created by Paul himself precisely to drive home the point that the Philippians should strive for unity by imitating the unselfishness of Christ. These scholars point out that the passage does not have the characteristics of either Greek or Hebrew poetry, that the sentences are structured in a way common to Paul, and that Paul breaks into this kind of "exalted prose" elsewhere in passages that cannot be hymnic quotations (e.g., 1 Cor. 1:22–25).[A-5]

Whether originally composed by Paul or not, 2:6–11 shows that from an early time Christians affirmed the preexistence of Christ, his equality with God, and his full humanity. The later explanation of these matters in the great ecumenical creeds of the fourth and fifth centuries were only developments of what the orthodox church believed from the first.

believers who, if they followed Jesus' example, would help one another in the troubles of life until that final day.

Selfish ambition . . . humility (2:3). Paul contrasts the greedy grasp for what one should not rightfully have (see comments on 1:17) with the humble willingness to put the needs of others first. The term "humility" often had bad overtones in ancient literature outside the New Testament. The Stoic philosopher Epictetus (A.D. 55–ca.135), for example, used it to refer to weakness of character.[32] Wherever the term appears in the New Testament, however, it carries a positive sense. Here Paul uses it to refer to a sacrificial willingness to give up one's rights and work for the good of others. The supreme example of this was Jesus, who "humbled himself" in obedience to God and suffered death by crucifixion (2:8).

Taking the very nature of a servant (2:7). The word translated "servant" in the NIV is the common word for "slave" (see comments on 1:1). But in what sense did Jesus take the form of a slave? From the standpoint of the Romans, Jesus was a common Jew, a member of a people whom the Roman general Pompey had conquered in 63 B.C. and over whom the Romans had ruled ever since, sometimes directly through governors and sometimes indirectly through puppet kings such as Herod the Great, his son Archelaeus, and his grandson Herod Agrippa I. From the Jewish perspective, however, rule by a foreign power was slavery—well-deserved punishment for breaking God's law (Deut. 28:68; Ezra 9:9). Jesus became just such a slave, sharing the curse of the law that had fallen on God's people (Gal. 3:10; 4:4), although he alone among God's people had broken none of God's laws.

Even death on a cross! (2:8). Opponents of Christianity regularly pointed out the scandal of the Christian worship of a crucified man. "God does not suffer, and God cannot be humiliated," smirked the second century anti-Christian philosopher Celsus.[33] Paul's gospel paints a different picture of God as he is revealed in Jesus Christ, however. Christ suffered not because he deserved it but because he selflessly refused to exploit his divinity and instead substituted his own death for the death of those who justly deserved God's wrath.

In heaven and on earth and under the earth (2:10). Ancient people often lived in fear of various invisible powers residing in the heavens and under the earth. Sometimes they attempted to defend themselves against these forces through the use of magic or sacrifices. The ancient geographer Strabo says that one morning off the coast of Sicily people saw the sea rise to a great height, smelled a noxious odor, and then saw flames, smoke, and mud emerge from the sea's surface to form an island. The governor of Sicily responded to this unnerving spectacle by sending a deputation to the newly created island so that sacrifices might be offered to turn aside the wrath of the gods who lived "under the earth" and in the sea.[34] The Philippians must have taken comfort in the knowledge that Jesus had triumphed over all inimical powers, and that every knee in heaven, on earth, and under the earth would one day, whether willingly or in subjection, bow before him and acknowledge him as Lord. As Peter puts it, Jesus "has gone into heaven and is at God's right hand—with angels, authorities, and powers in submission to him" (1 Peter 3:22; cf. Col. 1:22).

Do everything without complaining (2:14). The Greek word for "complaining" appears in only three other places in the New Testament, and this is its only appearance in Philippians. The Greek translators of the Old Testament often

---

▶ Crucifixion: The Slave's Punishment

Crucifixion was widely regarded in the ancient Roman world as "the slave's punishment" (*supplicium servile*). The victim of crucifixion served as a living public placard, warning all who passed by of what would happen to those who rebelled against their station in life, whether as a literal slave or as a member of a conquered, and therefore symbolically enslaved, nation. After the defeat of the rebellion under Spartacus (73 B.C.), in which many renegade slaves fought, six thousand prisoners were crucified.[A-6] Under Nero (emperor A.D. 54–68) a law was revived that allowed the crucifixion of all slaves within a household if their master had been murdered.[A-7] During the unrest in Judea following the death of Herod the Great, the Roman legate of Syria crucified two thousand Jews.[A-8] As the punishment reserved for slaves and the lower classes of conquered peoples, crucifixion was widely despised. The word was not even mentioned in polite company and was used by the lower classes, at least from the third century B.C. on, as a vulgar insult.[A-9]

used it, however, to refer to the "complaining" of the Israelites against Moses in the desert.[35] Paul may be making a subtle comparison between the disobedience of God's people under the old covenant and the dissension that apparently infected the Philippian church.[36]

Shine like stars in the universe (2:15). Israel was supposed to be "a light for the Gentiles" (Isa. 49:6; cf. 42:6–7), calling them to the worship of the one God. It failed in this vocation, however, and became itself a "warped and crooked generation" (Deut. 32:4–5). Here Paul calls on the Philippian church to drop their differences and to fulfill their calling as God's people.

Did not run . . . for nothing (2:16). Paul's metaphor of running is borrowed from the world of ancient athletics. He frequently used this kind of imagery to describe the strenuous nature of his apostolic labors and to stress that their reward lay in the future.[37] The Isthmian games were held every two years in Corinth, and Paul's many months of ministry in that city may have overlapped with the celebration of these games. Victorious athletes in the games received a crown of dry celery.[38] Like a runner in these games Paul focused all his energy on the goal that lay ahead (Phil. 3:13). The goal was the heavenly finish of his race (3:14), and the prize that awaited him he could variously describe as the imperishable crown of eternal life (1 Cor. 9:25), the crown of righteousness (2 Tim. 4:8), or the crown of his churches whom he hoped to present to God, blameless and pure, on that final day (Phil. 4:1; 1 Thess. 2:19).

Poured out like a drink offering (2:17). Many ancient cultures practiced sacrifi-

REFLECTIONS

WE OFTEN THINK OF THE PURITY of the church as more important than the peace of the church. Paul considered the church's purity important—chapter 3 shows that!—but he also recognized that needless disunity in Christ's body tarnishes the church's witness. A clear-headed understanding of the essentials of the gospel, derived from a deep level of familiarity with Scripture, will help us to tell the difference between sane and silly disagreements within the church.

cial rituals in which libations were poured over a slaughtered animal. In the Old Testament (e.g., Num. 15:1–10) libations are sometimes made in addition to other offerings rather than poured over them. Paul probably has the Old Testament model in mind here and speaks of how his own suffering and possible death joins with the sacrificial suffering (1:28) and giving (1:7; 2:26; 4:15–18) of the Philippians to make a sacrifice pleasing to God.

PHILIPPI

An inscription of a Byzantine-era cross from the remains of a basilica in the city.

The Travel Plans of Paul and His Coworkers (2:19–30)

Paul often refers in his letters to the movements of his coworkers and sometimes mentions his own travel plans also. This information can appear at the beginning of the letter, within its body, or at its conclusion. In Philippians, Paul has special reasons for locating his comments on Timothy and Epaphroditus right on the heels of his admonitions to unity in 2:1–18. These two coworkers provide examples of what it means to put the interests of others ahead of one's own interests. Paul wants the Philippians to turn from their "grumbling and complaining" against each other and to follow the path of unselfishness that these two valued friends have chosen.

You know that Timothy has proved himself (2:22). A more literal translation of this sentence might read, "His proven character you know." The noun rendered here as "proven character" (*dokimē*) refers to the quality of having remained faithful through difficult circumstances. The Jewish historian Josephus uses a verbal form of this word to describe how God put Abraham's faithfulness to the test when he commanded him to sacrifice his son Isaac.[39]

Epaphroditus . . . your messenger . . . to take care of my needs (2:25). Epaphroditus's mission was apparently twofold: to bring a financial gift from the Philippians to Paul (4:18) and to stay with Paul to care for him in prison. Roman prison officials made little, if any, provision for prisoners' food, clothing, bath, or bedding, and the meager amount of these basic necessities that the prisoner might receive had to be purchased at the prisoner's expense. Thus, prisoners were sometimes allowed to keep a small amount of money on them in prison and to receive gifts of food and clothing from friends and family.[40] The Philippians' concern that Paul would need these physical necessities seems to have been the primary reason that they sent Epaphroditus to him.

He was ill, and almost died (2:27). We can only speculate how and where Epaphroditus became ill. Did he contract

malaria as he traveled overland to the place of Paul's imprisonment? If he traveled by sea, did he become infected with disease by a fellow traveler in the close quarters of a Roman grain ship?[41] It is certainly possible that he became sick while tending to Paul's needs in prison. Ancient literature that refers to Roman imprisonment regularly mentions the "squalor of long captivity" (Lucan, 87 B.C.), "the squalor of the dungeon" (Cyprian, A.D. 250), and the appearance of prisoners as "foul and disfigured with filth and dirt" (Cyprian, A.D. 257).[42]

A Warning Against Theological Error (3:1–4:1)

If Paul was in prison in Ephesus when he wrote to the Philippians, then just before writing the letter he may have also written to the Galatians and to the Corinthians. In Galatians Paul appeals to several of his churches not to be convinced by a group of itinerant teachers that they must add observance of the Jewish law to faith in Christ in order to be acquitted before God's tribunal on the final day. In 1 Corinthians Paul battles against the notion, prominent in the Middle Platonism of the time, that the physical element of reality is to be shunned or demeaned but spiritual and intellectual elements are to be elevated to positions of primacy. In 3:1–4:1 Paul warns the Philippians against both errors, probably not because they had already infected the Philippian community, but because he hopes to prevent the problems he had encountered in Galatia and Corinth from cropping up in Philippi also.

Watch out for . . . dogs . . . men who do evil . . . mutilators of the flesh (3:2). The force of Paul's rhetoric in this statement

---

▶ Timothy Among Paul's Coworkers

Paul depended heavily for the success of his missionary labors on the help of a close circle of coworkers. Friends such as Priscilla, Aquila, and Apollos aided Paul in the proclamation of the gospel, in the establishment of his churches, and in earning enough income to provide practical support for his missionary work.[A-10] Occasionally coworkers such as Epaphroditus were his hands and feet while the apostle himself was in prison (Phil. 2:25; cf. Philem. 13). When relations between Paul and the Corinthians became strained, Titus carried Paul's "tearful letter" to Corinth (2 Cor. 2:1–14; 7:5–16). Later, while Paul labored in Macedonia, Titus traveled to Corinth again to encourage the Christians there to contribute to Paul's collection for the famine-plagued believers in Jerusalem (2 Cor. 8:16–24). In addition, he helped to organize Paul's newly established churches on Crete, freeing the apostle to work in other regions (Titus 1:5; 3:12).

Paul's most valued coworker, however, was Timothy. Paul had such confidence in him that he considered Timothy's presence in one of his churches as good as his own presence there. Thus, when Paul could not bear to think how the newly-established Thessalonian church might be faring in his absence, he sent Timothy to encourage them (1 Thess. 3:1–2). When the Corinthians began a downward spiral into dissension and immorality, Paul sent Timothy to remind them of Paul's "way of life in Christ Jesus" (1 Cor. 4:17; 16:10). Paul and Timothy were also close friends, as Paul's terms of endearment for his colleague reveal. Timothy is Paul's "beloved and faithful child in the Lord" (1 Cor. 4:17, RSV), his "true son in the faith" (1 Tim. 1:2), and his "dear son" (2 Tim. 1:2). Paul has no words of commendation for any of his coworkers more endearing, however, than his description of Timothy in Philippians 2:20–22.

is nearly impossible to communicate in English translation. In Greek, the statement consists of three clauses all beginning with the same verb ("watch out"!) and each verb's direct object begins with a "k" sound. We can almost catch the rhetorical effectiveness of the phrase with the translation, "Beware the curs! Beware the criminals! Beware the cutters!" Paul is referring to Jewish Christians who teach that circumcision, dietary observance, and Sabbath-keeping are all necessary requirements, in addition to faith in Christ, for salvation. By calling them "dogs" Paul is turning their own advocacy of ritual purity back upon them. Because ancient streets were often home to dogs (Ps 59:6, 14), who ate whatever they found, they may have been considered a symbol of nonobservance in matters of diet. The term "mutilators" (*katatomē*) is a play on the term "circumcision" (*peritomē*), which Paul uses in the next verse. Since circumcision was not necessary for salvation, those who promoted it were only mutilating the flesh, something that Leviticus 21:5 forbids as a pagan ritual.

No confidence in the flesh (3:3). Paul uses the term "flesh" here to mean any human credential that one might use to try to gain God's acceptance on the final day. The emphasis of his opponents on the fleshly rite of circumcision made it an especially appropriate metaphor.

Circumcised on the eighth day (3:5). The Mosaic law mandated the eighth day of life as the time for the circumcision of a male child (Gen. 17:12; Lev. 12:3), and although it involved work, this commandment was to take precedence over keeping the Sabbath (John 7:22–23). "Great is circumcision," said Rabbi Jose, "which overrides

even the rigor of the Sabbath."[43] Paul's circumcision on this day shows that he was not a proselyte but the son of observant Jews (cf. Luke 1:59; 2:21).[44]

Of the tribe of Benjamin (3:5). We know only from Acts that Paul also bore the Jewish name Saul. His namesake was the first king of Israel and the most famous member of the tribe of Benjamin.[45]

A Hebrew of Hebrews (3:5). The fourth-century bishop of Antioch John Chrysostom took this phrase to mean that Paul was raised to speak Aramaic, the native language of first-century Judaism, and most modern scholars believe that this is correct.[46]

In regard to the law, a Pharisee (3:5). The Jewish historian Josephus tells us that the Pharisees had the reputation of excelling all other Jews in the painstaking accuracy with which they interpreted the traditional laws of Judaism.[47] He also tells us that they wished to be righteous in everything.[48] We must not tar all Pharisees with the same brush, but these characteristics led some Pharisees to place confidence in themselves rather than in God (Luke 18:9). As a pre-Christian Pharisee, Paul had placed his confidence in what he calls "a righteousness of my own" (3:9). He seems to have thought that his own status and efforts were good enough to play some part in his acquittal on the final day.

As for zeal, persecuting the church (3:6). Paul identifies himself here and in Galatians 1:13–14 with a tradition of zealotry in Judaism that stretches back to Simeon and Levi (Gen. 34), Phinehas (Num. 25), and Elijah (1 Kings 18–19). Its chief characteristic was a concern for the Jewish law so intense that it could sometimes be expressed as violence against anyone who opposed it. Zeal for the law, for example, drove Mattathias Maccabeus to take up arms against the vast Seleucid army in the second century B.C. (1 Macc. 2:27).[49] The pre-Christian Paul probably persecuted the church because of its willingness to admit Gentiles to the people of God apart from conformity to the Mosaic law. He correctly saw that the gospel implied the end of the law as a boundary marker for the people of God, but incorrectly believed that this development was not from God.[50]

Profit . . . loss (3:7). The terms "profit" and "loss" are financial terms. They could be used in a legal setting to speak of the injured party's "loss" that had become the criminal's "gain."[51]

The righteousness that comes from God (3:9). Paul believed that in Jesus Christ God had effected the final display of his righteous, saving activity on behalf of his people. He had done this through Christ's death on the cross (Rom. 3:21–26), where he exchanged Christ's righteousness for our sinfulness (2 Cor. 5:21). On the cross, to use Jeremiah's phrase, the Lord had become "Our Righteousness" (Jer. 23:6).

Already been made perfect (3:12). Striving for perfection through intellectual and spiritual enlightenment was a common religious ideal in Greco-Roman antiquity. Those who responded positively to the preaching of this message "became perfect men, since they had received a complete mind."[52] Paul had seen such ideas infect the church at Corinth, where some believers claimed that they had already been perfected by their spiritual knowledge and

denied the goodness of the physical world. He would encounter this "knowledge which is falsely so called" (1 Tim. 6:20 ASV) again at Ephesus. Here in Philippians he is perhaps taking precautions against the misinterpretation of Philippians 3:7–11 as support for such false teaching.

I press on toward the goal to win the prize (3:14). The imagery of this verse comes from the athletic arena (see comments on 2:16), where runners would fix their eyes on the post that marked the end point of the race and winners received a prize. The term "goal" was often used figuratively of an object on which one could fix his or her eyes and so be guided safely to a final destination. In the third-century B.C. *Letter of Aristeas*, for example, the author says that "life is rightly guided when the pilot knows the *goal* toward which he must make his way" (251).[53]

Enemies of the cross of Christ (3:18). Opponents of Christianity in antiquity regularly mocked Christians for their worship of a man who had died by crucifixion. The early Christian apologist Minucius Felix puts these words on the lips of an imaginary, but typical, opponent: "To say that their ceremonies centre

---

R E F L E C T I O N S

IT IS WORTH ASKING FROM TIME TO TIME WHERE OUR confidence lies. Do we think that God loves us because of all that we do for him—teaching Sunday school, ministering to the poor, serving in the offices of the church? Or do we know that God loves us—regardless of what we do—because of what he has done for us on the cross of Jesus Christ? If our confidence before God lies in anything but his love for us, we have made the mistake of the pre-Christian Paul, and like him, we need to trust solely in the righteousness that comes from God for our salvation.

on a man put to death for his crime and on the fatal wood of the cross is to assign to these abandoned wretches sanctuaries which are appropriate to them and the kind of worship they deserve."[54] Under such circumstances some Christians succumbed to the temptation to play down the significance of Christ's crucifixion (see, for example, 1 John 5:6). Paul's emphasis on the folly of the cross in 1 Corinthians 1:18–2:5 may mean that the Corinthians were moving in this direction, and here in Philippians 3:18 he seems to be taking precautions against such influences among the Philippians.

Our citizenship is in heaven (3:20). The word translated "citizenship" (*politeuma*) was sometimes used generally to speak of the political rights of a particular group. The third-century Macedonian King Philip V, for example, commented that the Romans, when they freed their slaves, welcomed them "into *citizenship*." The same word could also refer to a distinct ethnic group that lived away from its homeland and was governed by its own constitution—"a city within a city."[55] An inscription from the town of Bernike in Cyrenaica, for example, speaks of "the *community* of Jews in Bernike" (13 B.C.), and the third-century B.C. *Letter of Aristeas* can speak of a group of Jews in Egypt as "some from the Jewish *community*."[56] Here Paul reminds the Philippians that although they have been marginalized by the society in which they live, they are not people without a country. They form a distinct group with its own loyalties, its own homeland (see also comments on 1:27), and, as we see below, its own "Savior."

We eagerly await a Savior from there (3:20). In Hellenistic and Roman society, the ruler was frequently called "savior." This term was especially common for Roman emperors. Plutarch says that the Greeks use "the designation 'savior'" for the ruler because of his accomplishments (*De Coriolano* 11).[57] Thus, an inscription from Ephesus dated to A.D. 48, only a few years before Paul wrote Philippians, speaks of Julius Caesar as "a visible god and political savior of human life." Another inscription from Egypt, this time perhaps from a few years after Philippians, calls Emperor Nero "savior and benefactor of the world." Paul wants the Philippians to know that the "Savior" of their "community" (*politeuma*, see above) is none other than Jesus, who will bring "everything under his control" (3:21; cf. 2:10).[58]

▶ God's Righteousness in Paul's Bible

Paul's Bible was filled with references to God's willingness to rescue his covenant people from peril. It sometimes referred to this saving work as God's "righteousness." For example, the psalmist says, "The LORD has made his salvation known and revealed his righteousness to the nations. He has remembered his love and his faithfulness to the house of Israel" (Ps. 98:2–3a). Occasionally, the Scriptures refer to a righteous king through whom God will act decisively and finally for the good of his people. Jeremiah, for example, prophesies, "'The days are coming,' declares the LORD, 'when I will raise up to David a righteous Branch, a King who will reign wisely and do what is just and right in the land.... This is the name by which he will be called: The LORD Our Righteousness'" (Jer. 23:5–6).[A-11]

My . . . crown (4:1). This is probably a metaphorical reference to the wreath of dry celery worn by athletes after they had reached their goal and won the race (see comments on 2:16 and 3:14).

Concluding Admonitions (4:2–9)

Near the end of several letters Paul includes a section of short, pithy exhortations similar to what we find here. For example, Paul draws his first letter to the Thessalonians to a close with a series of brief admonitions to respect the church's leaders, to live in peace with each other, to be joyful, to pray, to be thankful, to be sensitive to the Spirit, to listen to prophecies, to test everything, to hold on to what is good, and to avoid evil (1 Thess. 5:12–22). Here in Philippians, he calls the names of some of his readers for the first time (Phil. 4:2–3) and applies the admonitions to unity in 1:27–2:30 specifically to a dispute between Euodia and Syntyche. In addition, he employs but modifies an Epicurean philosophical convention to summarize for his readers the attitude that they should have toward the persecution they are facing (cf. 1:27–30).

Contended at my side (4:3). This phrase translates a word (*synathleō*) that in Greek is a compound of the preposition "with" (*syn*) and a verb that can mean "to contend in battle" or "to compete in athletic games" (*athleō*).[59] Paul is probably continuing to use the athletic imagery that has appeared so often in his previous argument (2:16; 3:13–14; 4:1).

Loyal yokefellow (4:3). At least since the early third-century church father Clement of Alexandria, some people have thought that Paul was addressing his wife with this phrase (*Miscellanies* 3.6). The word "yokefellow" (*syzygos* in Greek) can mean "wife," but that cannot be its meaning here since Paul qualifies the word with the masculine form of the adjective "loyal" (*gnesie*). If Paul were referring to his wife, he would have used the feminine form of the adjective (*gnesia*).[60]

Fellow workers (4:3). This is the term Paul uses for Timothy, Epaphroditus, Titus, Prisca (Priscilla in Acts), Aquila, Apollos, and others who formed the inner circle of his helpers (see "Timothy Among Paul's Coworkers," above). Paul's language implies that Euodia and Syntyche were members of this group. How did they have the leisure to contend at Paul's side in the cause of the gospel? We cannot know definitely, but Euodia and Syntyche may have been wealthy women, like Lydia (Acts 16:14), who naturally assumed positions of prominence in the Philippian church because they had held some position of responsibility commensurate with their social rank in the political or religious institutions of Philippi prior to their conversion. Euodia and Syntyche are both Greek names, and at least in Asia, Greek women sometimes held important political positions.[61] In Philippi, women probably occupied leading roles in the worship of the goddess Diana.[62]

The book of life (4:3). The Old Testament sometimes refers to a record, kept by God, of those who belong to God's people. Moses pleads with God to blot his own name from it rather than the names of the rebellious desert generation of Israelites (Ex. 32:32–33). David calls it "the book of life" (Ps. 69:28), and Isaiah carries the idea into the future when he speaks of the blessings that will come to those "who are recorded among the living in Jerusalem" at the time of the restoration of God's people (Isa. 4:3). John frequently refers to a "book of life," kept by Jesus himself, that contains the names of those who belong to God's people and will be citizens of the heavenly Jerusalem.[63] Probably lying in the background of all these references is the civic practice of record-keeping; the names of citizens were commonly recorded on lists in antiquity.[64] Thus, in the command of the Macedonian King Philip V referred to above (see comments on Phil. 3:20), Philip tells the city officials of Larisa to restore to the "community" the names that they have erased, apparently from some list of citizens.[65] By using the phrase "book of life" here, Paul may be reminding his Philippian coworkers that although their status as good citizens of Philippi is in jeopardy, they are nevertheless enrolled on the citizen list of God's heavenly society.[66]

Let your gentleness be evident to all (4:5). The term "gentleness" was often used to describe an attitude of kindness where a normal response would be retaliation. Thus in the apocryphal book Wisdom of Solomon, a group of evil people decide to persecute a righteous man whose virtuous life is a rebuke to them. "Let us test him with insult and torture," they say, "so that we may find out his *gen-*

tleness, and make trial of his forbearance."[67] This is probably also the nuance of the term in 2 Corinthians 10:1, where Paul implies that the origin of his own gentle conduct with the recalcitrant Corinthians is "the meekness and *gentleness* of Christ." Similarly, Paul wants the persecuted Philippians (Phil. 1:28–29) to return evil with good (cf. Rom. 12:21).

Think about such things (4:8). Ancient moral philosophers often consoled those who were grieving or otherwise plagued with difficult circumstances to turn their minds away from their difficulties (*avocatio*) and to turn them to pleasurable or virtuous thoughts (*revocatio*). Epicureans (see comments on 1:12) advocated turning one's thoughts from the painful to the pleasurable. Stoics, such as Cicero and Seneca, advocated replacing painful thoughts with the contemplation of virtue. Cicero's list of virtues for contemplation is similar to Paul's list here: "all that is lovely, honourable, of good report."[68] Paul may have taken over this convention and, varying the approach represented by Cicero and Seneca, advocated that the Philippians commit the worries that accompany their persecution in prayer to God (4:6) and turn their minds to the contemplation of the virtues.[69]

A Word of Thanks (4:10–20)

Paul draws his letter to a close with an expression of appreciation for the Philippians' gift to him through Epaphroditus. Paul's use of financial metaphors in this part of the letter (4:15–18) implies that the gift consisted primarily of money, although it may have included clothes and other basic necessities that would ease the harsh conditions of his imprisonment (see comments on 2:25). Whereas Paul is clearly appreciative of these gifts (4:10, 14–16, 18–20), he qualifies his thanks in vv. 11–13 by saying that he really did not need them and in v. 17 that he did not seek them. He did not want the Philippians to think either that he preached the gospel for money or that they were the benefactors of his ministry.

Content (4:11). This word translates a widely discussed virtue in ancient Greek moral philosophy (*autarkēs*). Aristotle defined contentment as "possessing all things and needing nothing."[70] The word became especially important to the Stoics, among whom it represented the highest of Stoic ideals—complete self-sufficiency. Marcus Aurelius, who describes his adoptive father as the ideal Stoic man, claims that he was "self-sufficient in all things."[71] Paul's understanding

of contentment could hardly have been more different from this. He was content not because he needed nothing or because he was self-sufficient, but because he was utterly dependent on a God who gave him everything he truly needed. Through Paul's suffering God had taught the apostle, "My grace is sufficient for you, for my power is made perfect in weakness" (2 Cor. 12:9).[72]

The matter of giving and receiving (4:15). These are common financial terms for credit (*dosis*) and debit (*lēmpsis*). Sirach 42:7, for example, advises, "Whatever you deal out, let it be by number and weight, and make a record of all that you give out [*dosis*] or take in [*lēmpsis*]." The language was sometimes used metaphorically among friends to refer to the mutual "give" and "take" of friendship. These connotations probably lie beneath

▶ Sophistry, Philosophy, and Chicanery in the Greco-Roman World

Giving material wealth, especially to teachers and lecturers, was fraught with significance in ancient Greco-Roman society. For example, the group of itinerant teachers known as "Sophists" charged a fee for teaching their pupils how to succeed in life. Their lectures ran the gamut of self-help topics from memory improvement to effective oratory. All Sophists were skilled speakers and many had an impressive physical presence, often enhanced by a stunning wardrobe. Their trade was frequently lucrative, and although there were exceptions, their profession was somewhat cynically oriented toward a life of material success irrespective of any search for truth.[A-12]

Although less impressive in outward appearance and more oriented toward the pursuit of truth, Cynic philosophers also depended on the generosity of benefactors to support their life of itinerant philosophical teaching. Not infrequently the ability

of con artists to ape the costume and manner of Cynic teachers enabled them to defraud the gullible of considerable sums and then to leave town without a trace. The second-century satirist Lucian parodied these swindlers in his play The Runaways. "They collect tribute," he says, "going from house to house, or, as they themselves express it, they 'shear the sheep': and they expect many to give, either out of respect for their cloth or for fear of their abusive language" (14).[A-13]

Paul's reserved expression of thanks in Philippians may be an effort to distance himself both from any hint that his teaching is motivated by a desire for financial gain and from the possibility that the Philippians were his benefactors. Paul preached the gospel not for money but because God had called him to preach (1 Cor. 9:15–18), and his authority as an apostle came from no human being but from God himself (Gal. 1:1).[A-14]

Paul's use of the language here since Paul's point is that he had entered into a unique relationship with the Philippians: He had allowed no other church but theirs to give financial support to his Gentile mission (2 Cor. 11:8–9). Elsewhere Paul had worked with his hands for his own support (1 Cor. 4:12; 2 Thess. 3:7–10).[73]

I have received full payment (4:18). Paul is again using technical commercial language for writing a receipt of payment. One example of the literal financial use of this language—and it could be multiplied many times—comes from an ostracon dated A.D. 32–33 and stating that Pamaris the son of Hermodorus has "received full payment" from a man named Abos of a tax levied on aliens in the city of Thebes.[74]

Conclusion (4:21–23)

Letters to friends and family in ancient times typically contained a simple conclusion, often using nothing more than the word "farewell" (*errōso*). Occasionally, however, especially in letters from the first century, the conclusion was expanded to include a brief wish for the health of the recipient.[75] Sometimes conclusions included greetings to third parties and greeted the recipient on behalf of someone in the sender's company. The soldier Apollinarios writes to his mother, for example, and closes the letter this way: "I greet (salute) my brothers much, and Apollinarios and his children, and Karalas and his children. I greet Ptolemy, and Ptolemais and her children. I greet all your friends, each by name. I pray that you are well."[76] And in a letter written within a few years of the time Paul wrote Philippians, Herennia concludes a letter to her father Pompeius with best wishes "to Charitous and her children" and greetings from Herennia's younger brother, "Pompeius junior."[77] Paul follows the same custom in Philippians, sending greetings to all the Philippian Christians and greeting them on behalf of everyone with him (4:21).

Especially those who belong to Caesar's household (4:22). The phrase "Caesar's household" refers to slaves and freed slaves who served the emperor either as part of his entourage of personal attendants in Rome or as part of the more widely dispersed group of servants who supervised his financial affairs. Both groups were proud of the status that their work in the emperor's service accorded them, and they often added to their names an abbreviation showing that they were slaves or freedmen of the emperor.[78] Paul may intend these greetings as an encouragement to the persecuted Philippians that he knows of people even within the structures of imperial power who have been touched by the gospel.

REFLECTIONS

PAUL COULD BE CONTENT EVEN IN PRISON BECAUSE he was content when the gospel was making progress, and the gospel was making progress because of his imprisonment (1:12). Paul could also be content when other preachers of the gospel increased his suffering. "What does it matter?" he says, "the important thing is that Christ is preached" (1:18). When we are discontent, perhaps we should ask ourselves where the origin of contentment lies for us. Does it lie in the progress of the gospel (if so, we need never fear that God will fail to see it progress) or does it lie in physical comfort or emotional security?

ANNOTATED BIBLIOGRAPHY

Bockhuehl, Markus. *The Epistle to the Philippians*. BNTC. Peabody, Mass.: Hendrickson, 1998.

A well-written, concise exposition marked by insights from both Jewish and Greco-Roman sources and informed by a mastery of the best social and cultural studies of ancient Philippi.

Bruce, F. F. *Philippians*. GNC. New York: Harper & Row, 1983.

A short, lucid explanation of the letter with frequent insights from the history and culture of Paul's time.

Caird, G. B. *Paul's Letters from Prison (Ephesians, Philippians, Colossians, Philemon) in the Revised Standard Version*. Oxford: Oxford University Press, 1976.

A brilliant exposition of Philippians within only a few pages, from the author of the classic *The Language and Imagery of the Bible*.

Fee, Gordon D. *Paul's Letter to the Philippians*. NICNT. Grand Rapids: Eerdmans, 1995.

A sound exposition of the letter with constant reference to its character as an ancient letter of friendship, to its effectiveness as an effort at oral communication, and to its theological significance for the present-day church.

Hawthorne, Gerald F. *Philippians*. WBC. Waco, Tex.: Word, 1983.

An insightful exposition of the Greek text by a revered and erudite professor of the Greek language.

Martin, Ralph P. *Philippians*. NCBC. Grand Rapids/London: Eerdmans/Marshall, Morgan & Scott, 1976.

A short, clear, and exegetically sane exposition, based on the RSV.

Murphy-O'Connor, Jerome. *Paul: A Critical Life*. Oxford: Clarendon, 1996.

Although sullied by its skeptical attitude toward the historicity of Acts, its truncated Pauline canon, and its frequent speculativeness, this book is filled with rich insights on the historical and cultural background of Paul's ministry.

O'Brien, Peter T. *The Epistle to the Philippians: A Commentary on the Greek Text*. NIGTC. Grand Rapids: Eerdmans, 1991.

The most detailed exposition of the Greek text in over a century and a reliable guide to virtually every exegetical problem in the letter.

Rapske, Brian. *Paul in Roman Custody*. Grand Rapids: Eerdmans, 1994.

A gripping account of every facet of ancient imprisonment with special attention to the record of Paul's imprisonments in Acts.

Silva, Moisés. *Philippians*. BECNT. Grand Rapids: Baker, 1992.

A theologically sensitive explanation of the letter with sound insights into the meaning of the text from the field of linguistics.

Thielman, Frank. *Philippians*. NIVAC. Grand Rapids: Zondervan, 1995.

A commentary that focuses both on the original meaning and on the application of this letter of Paul.

White, John L. *Light from Ancient Letters*. Foundations & Facets: New Testament. Philadelphia: Fortress, 1986.

A collection of 117 ancient papyrus letters from Egypt and an illuminating account of how and why they were written.

Witherington, Ben III. *Friendship and Finances in Philippi: The Letter of Paul to the Philippians*. The New Testament in Context. Valley Forge, Pa.: Trinity Press International, 1994.

A clearly written exposition of the Philippians in light of ancient rhetorical and cultural conventions.

Main Text Notes

1. David W. J. Gill and Conrad Gempf, *The Book of Acts in Its Graeco–Roman Setting* (Grand Rapids: Eerdmans, 1994), 401.
2. See Richard S. Ascough, "Civic Pride at Philippi: The Text–Critical Problem of Acts 16.12," *NTS* 44 (1998): 93–103.
3. Appian, *Civil Wars* 4.13.105–32.
4. Strabo, *Geogr.* 7.41; Dio Cassius, *Roman History* 51.4.6.
5. Holland L. Hendrix, "Philippi," *ABD*, 5:315.
6. Ibid., 315.
7. Nils Martin Persson Nilsson, Herbert Jennings Rose, and Charles Martin Robertson, "Dionysius," *OCD*², 352–53; Hendrix, "Philippi," 5:315.
8. Valerie Abrahamsen, "Christianity and the Rock Reliefs at Philippi," *BA* 51 (1988): 48–50.
9. Ibid., 51.
10. Gill and Gempf, *Greco–Roman Setting*, 412; cf. Markus Bockmuehl, *The Epistle to the Philippians* (BNTC; Peabody, Mass.: Hendrickson, 1998), 6–8.
11. As suggested by Paul Collart, *Philippes: Ville de Macédoine* (Paris: École française d'Athènes, 1937), 323, 458–60. But see Peter Pilheifer, *Philippi* (WUNT 87; Tübingen: Mohr, 1995), 167–74.
12. Stanley K. Stowers, *Letter Writing in Greco-Roman Antiquity* (LEC 5; Louisville, Ky.: Westminster/John Knox, 1986), 66.
13. MM, 244.
14. Ibid., 149.
15. A. Weiser, "διακονέω," *EDNT*, 1:302.
16. Arland J. Hultgren, *Paul's Gospel and Mission: The Outlook from His Letter to the Romans* (Philadelphia: Fortress, 1985), 21–26.
17. On "confirming" (*bebaiōsis*) see BAGD, 138, and MM, 108.
18. John L. White, *Light from Ancient Letters* (Philadelphia: Fortress, 1986), 104.
19. Ibid., 173.
20. Plato, *Menexenus* 245*d*.
21. Ceslas Spicq, *TLNT*, 1:420–23.
22. *Letter of Aristeas* 210.
23. White, *Light from Ancient Letters*, 158.
24. Quoted in Cicero, *On the Ends of Goods and Evils* 2.30.96.
25. cf. Cicero, *Tusculan Disputations* 3.16.35–3.17.38; cf. 5.23.6.
26. I am indebted for these insights to Paul A. Holloway, "*Bona Cogitare*: An Epicurean Consolation in Phil 4:8–9," *HTR* 91 (1998): 89–96.
27. Brian Rapske, *The Book of Acts and Paul in Roman Custody* (Grand Rapids: Eerdmans, 1994), 20–35; Ignatius, *Romans* 5.1.
28. Ibid., 290.
29. Spicq, *TLNT*, 2:70–71.
30. J. A. O. Larsen, "Roman Greece," in *An Economic Survey of Ancient Rome*, ed. Tenney Frank (Baltimore: Johns Hopkins Univ. Press, 1933–40), 4:459.
31. Elthelbert Stauffer, "ἀγών," *TDNT*, 1:136; *4 Macc.* 11:20; 16:16; 17:10–16.
32. Walter Grundmann, "ταπεινός," *TDNT*, 8:5; Epictetus, *Discourses* 3.24.56.
33. Celsus, *On the True Doctrine: A Discourse Against the Christians* (New York: Oxford Univ. Press, 1987), 107.
34. Strabo, *Geogr.* 6.2.11.
35. Ex. 16:2–9; 17:3; Num. 11:1; cf. 14:2.
36. Phil. 4:2; cf. 1 Cor. 10:1–13.
37. 1 Cor. 9:24–27; 2 Tim. 4:6–8; cf. Gal. 2:2.
38. Jerome Murphy-O'Connor, *Paul: A Critical Life* (Oxford: Clarendon, 1996), 259.
39. *Ant.* 1.13.4 §233; cf. Gen. 22:1–19; Spicq, *TLNT*, 1:355.
40. Rapske, *Paul in Roman Custody*, 196–97, 209–19.
41. On the many dangers that ancient travelers faced, see Murphy-O'Connor, *Paul*, 96–101.
42. Rapske, *Paul in Roman Custody*, 217.
43. The translation is from Herbert Danby, *The Mishnah* (Oxford: Oxford Univ. Press, 1933), 268; *m. Nedarim* 3.11.
44. Peter T. O'Brien, *Commentary on Philippians* (NIGTC; Grand Rapids: Eerdmans, 1991), 369.
45. 1 Sam. 9:21; 10:20–21; 2 Sam. 21:14.
46. Chrysostom, *Homilies on Philippians* 10.
47. Josephus, *Life* 38 §191; *J.W.* 2.8.14 §162.
48. Josephus, *Ant.* 18.1.3 §15.
49. Terence L. Donaldson, *Paul and the Gentiles: Remapping the Apostle's Convictional World* (Minneapolis: Fortress, 1997), 285–86.
50. Ibid., 273–92.
51. Aristotle, *Nicomachean Ethics* 5.4, 1132a.
52. C. K. Barrett, *The New Testament Background: Selected Documents* (rev. and exp. ed.; San Francisco: HarperCollins, 1987), 101; *Corpus Hermeticum* 4; *The Bowl* 3–7.
53. See MM, 579.
54. Martin Hengel, *Crucifixion* (Philadelphia: Fortress, 1977), 1–10: Minucius Felix, *Octavius* 9.

55. E. Mary Smallwood, *The Jews under Roman Rule from Pompey to Diocletian: A Study in Political Relations* (Leiden: Brill, 1981), 225.

56. MM, 525–26. See also Smallwood, *Jews under Roman Rule*, 225–30.

57. Werner Foerster, "σωτήρ," *TDNT*, 7:1007.

58. MM, 621–22.

59. LSJ, 32.

60. Murphy-O'Connor, *Paul*, 64.

61. Ben Witherington III, *Friendship and Finances in Philippi: The Letter of Paul to the Philippians* (The New Testament in Context; Valley Forge, Pa.: Trinity Press International, 1994), 108.

62. Abrahamsen, "Christianity and the Rock Reliefs at Philippi," 46–56.

63. E.g., Rev. 20:12, 15; 21:27.

64. H. Balz, "βιβλίον," *EDNT*, 1:218.

65. MM, 525.

66. Gerald Hawthorne, *Philippians* (WBC 43; Waco, Tex.: Word, 1983), 181.

67. Wisd. Sol. 2:19 RSV modified.

68. Cicero, *Tusc. Disp.* 5.23.67; The translation is from the Loeb Classical Library edition of Cicero's works.

69. I am indebted for these insights to Holloway, "*Bona Cogitare*," 89–96.

70. Aristotle, *Politics* 7.5, 1326b; Gerhard Kittel, "αὐτάρκεια," *TDNT*, 1:466–67.

71. Marcus Aurelius, *Meditations* 1.16.11; J. N. Sevenster, *Paul and Seneca* (Leiden: E. J. Brill, 1961), 114.

72. B. Siede, "Suffice, Satisfy," *NIDNTT*, 3:728.

73. Gordon D. Fee, *Paul's Letter to the Philippians* (NICNT; Grand Rapids: Eerdmans, 1995), 439–47.

74. Adolf Deissmann, *Light from the Ancient East* (Grand Rapids: Baker, 1978 [reprt.]), 111.

75. White, *Light from Ancient Letters*, 199–200.

76. Ibid., 196.

77. Ibid., 141.

78. P. R. C. Weaver, *Familia Caesaris: A Social Study of the Emperor's Freedmen and Slaves* (Cambridge: Cambridge Univ. Press, 1972), 1–8.

Sidebar and Chart Notes

A-1. Henry Michael Denne Parker and George Ronald Watson, "Praetorians," *OCD²*, 873–74.

A-2. Anthony A. Barrett, *Caligula: The Corruption of Power* (New Haven, Conn.: Yale Univ. Press, 1989), 172–74.

A-3. See Abrahamsen, "Christianity and the Rock Reliefs at Philippi," 51.

A-4. Ralph P. Martin, *A Hymn of Christ: Philippians 2:5–11 in Recent Interpretation and in the Setting of Early Christian Worship* (Downers Grove, Ill.: InterVarsity, 1997), 24–41.

A-5. Gordon Fee, "Philippians 2:5–11: Hymn or Exalted Pauline Prose?" *BBR* 2 (1992): 29–46.

A-6. Caesar, *Civil Wars* 1.120.

A-7. Tacitus, *Ann.* 13.32.1; Martin Hengel, *Crucifixion*, 51–63.

A-8. Josephus, *Ant.* 17.10.10 §295.

A-9. Ibid., 9–10.

A-10. Acts 18:2–4, 18, 24–28; Rom. 16:3–9; 1 Cor. 3:9.

A-11. See Hultgren, *Paul's Gospel and Mission*, 12–46.

A-12. See Guy Cromwell Field, "Sophists," *OCD²*, 1000, and Bruce W. Winter, "Is Paul Among the Sophists?" *RTR* 53 (1994): 28–29.

A-13. The translation is from the Loeb Classical Library edition of Lucian's works.

A-14. See the helpful discussion in Witherington, *Friendship and Finances*, 123–24.

COLOSSIANS

by Clinton E. Arnold

The City of Colosse

Colosse was a small agrarian town in western Asia Minor (modern Turkey).[1] It was located about 120 miles east of Ephesus in the Lycus River Valley of the territory of Phrygia. The city lay near the base of Mount Cadmus (elevation 8,435 feet) and was only eleven miles southeast of Laodicea.

Because of the sparse historical records, we have no way of determining the approximate size of the city. We do know that Colosse was rather insignificant in Roman history; it is mentioned only by a handful of writers. The city was largely overshadowed by the larger and more prosperous Laodicea. Even nearby Hierapolis (fifteen miles northwest) figures more prominently in the historical record.

The distinctive color of the wool produced at Colosse, commonly called *colossinus,* aided the success of the textile industry there. The economic position of the city was

COLOSSE

Alongside the tel of the ancient city.

▶ Colossians
IMPORTANT FACTS:

- **AUTHOR:** The apostle Paul and Timothy.
- **DATE:** A.D. 60–62 (Paul imprisoned in Rome).
- **OCCASION:**
  - To warn believers about the dangers of a spiritualistic teaching being pushed by some influential people in the church.
  - To provide positive Christian teaching to facilitate the spiritual growth of the Colossian believers.
- **KEY THEMES:**
  1. The supremacy of Christ over all of creation, especially the powers.
  2. Believers participate with Christ in his death, resurrection, and fullness.

also enhanced by its location on the major trade route leading from the Aegean coast (to the west) to the heartland of Asia Minor and on to Syria and the east.

There is evidence of a sizeable Jewish population in the area around Colosse, and thus probably in the city of Colosse. This is based on a reference in Cicero to the amount of tax collected for the Jerusalem temple from this district in the first century B.C.[2] No synagogue has yet been discovered.

Two different ancient writers attest to a severe earthquake that rocked this region in the early 60s of the first century A.D.[3] Laodicea suffered extensive damage, and we can only surmise that Colosse suffered the same. It appears that the quake may have struck shortly after Paul wrote his letter to the church. Paul's eloquent words about Christ as Lord of creation must have been especially meaningful to the believers after this tragic event.

Archaeological Prospects at Colosse

COLOSSE AND EPHESUS

Colosse was about 100 miles due east of Ephesus.

▼

Colosse has never been excavated, although groups have applied to the Turkish government for permission. The site was discovered in 1835 by explorer W. J. Hamilton. Members of the Near East Archaeological Society and others have conducted site surveys, which have yielded evidence of an acropolis, a theater on the south bank of the Lycus River, a necropolis (a graveyard), and the remains of other ancient buildings on the northern bank of the river.[4] The excavation of Colosse could yield important finds with implications for the interpretation of the letter. This is particularly important because of the influence of local religious traditions on the teaching of the faction that Paul opposes in the letter. The excavation of temples and discovery of religious inscriptions would provide helpful insight about the nature of these cults and the folk religious beliefs of the area. Of course, any discoveries of Jewish inscriptions or symbols would greatly assist in clarifying the picture of what Judaism was like in this area.

The Spiritual Climate of the Area

Because of the nature of the problem facing the Colossian church, it is important to have an awareness of some of the spiritual beliefs of the people living in this area who became Christians. There were no secular humanists at this time. In fact, most of the people living in this country area could aptly be described as animists. They believed in the reality of the gods and goddesses as well as in the pervasive influence of good and evil spirits. Here are a few specific features of their beliefs that will help to better understand the nature of the issue the church is struggling with:

A religiously pluralistic environment. Like any other city in the Roman empire

COLOSSE
The north side of
the unexcavated
tel.

at this time, Colosse was religiously pluralistic. We know this because of the variety of gods and goddesses depicted on a few coins that have been discovered originally minted in the city.[5] They suggest that among the deities the Colossians worshiped were the Ephesian Artemis, the Laodicean Zeus, Artemis (the huntress), the local moon-god Men, the lunar goddess Selene, the Egyptian deities Isis and Sarapis, as well as a number of well-known Greek divinities, including Athena, Demeter, Hygieia, Helios, and Tyche. It is likely that other distinctively Asia Minor deities would have been worshiped there as well, such as the mother goddess, Cybele, and the goddess of witchcraft, Hekate.

Blending of religious beliefs. It was common for a person at this time not only to worship more than one god or goddess (polytheism), but also for the religions themselves to reflect a borrowing of ideas and forms of worship from one another. Such a blending of religious ideas is called *syncretism*.

A strong belief in dangerous spirits and powers. In their belief, not all gods, goddesses, and spirits were benevolent. Most were to be feared. Even the good deities, if offended, could manifest their anger toward the people in some kind of disaster. People also had to worry about the potential of being cursed (and not in the sense of someone uttering a four-letter word at them). In this context, curses involved the summoning of supernatural beings to harm the life of another person. Archaeologists have discovered curse tablets in Asia Minor that illustrate these dark arts.[6]

The people also feared the many spirits associated with the wildlife, agriculture, and the intersection of roads. Spirits were associated with some objects that could pose a significant threat to one's safety. They believed that astral spirits, the zodiac, planetary deities, and the constellations (such as Pleiades and the constellation of the bear—Arktos) held sway over fate and influenced the affairs of day-to-day life. They were also fearful of the underworld and the gods and goddesses such as Hades and Hekate. Not least, they had to be wary of the spirits of deceased ancestors and of the untimely dead who haunted and could wreak terror.

An appeal to "angels" and other divine beings for protection. There is abundant evidence that people in Asia Minor tended to invoke various spirit beings for protection and deliverance.[7] Numerous inscriptions have been discovered in the area illustrating the fact that people called on angels for help. This was true in the pagan cults and in Judaism.

Ecstatic forms of worship. One final aspect of the religious practice of the area is the manifestation of extreme forms of

GREEK INSCRIPTION

This inscription from nearby Hierapolis mentions the goddess Tyche.

▼

behavior in the context of worship. This often led to the abuse of the body. This is best illustrated by the nature of the worship directed to the Great Mother goddess of Asia Minor, Cybele, and her consort, Attis. Worshipers often engaged in rites of self-mutilation and flagellation.[8] We may also add to this the fact that fasting and other forms of self-denial were a part of the preparation for initiation into some of the mystery cults in the region.

The Introduction of Christianity to the City

In the mid–50s, the apostle Paul spent considerable time in the city of Ephesus. Luke informs us that during this time all "Asia heard the word of the Lord" (Acts 19:10). This was the most likely time that a man named Epaphras journeyed from Colosse to Ephesus, heard Paul's preaching about the Messiah Jesus, became a Christian, and was instructed in the way of the Lord by Paul. This new believer then returned to his home city and zealously spread the news about Christ. If he was a Jew, which seems probable, he would have gone immediately into the synagogue(s) and proclaimed Christ. Here a number of Jews and many Gentile "God-fearers" and proselytes (Gen-

---

▶ Plutarch's *Dread of the Gods*

Plutarch, a well-known first-century writer, wrote an entire essay on the common fear of the gods among the common people of the Roman empire. In *Deisidaimonia* (*Dread of the Gods*), Plutarch describes how the people are terrified by the gods and worried about potential attacks by evil spirits.[A-1] They experience awful dreams and see frightening and horrible apparitions. They also live in the fear of life beyond the grave, imagining that they will descend to the abysmal underworld and face countless numbers of woes. This dread prompts people to wear protective amulets and to use magical charms and spells, to seek the assistance of magicians and conjurers, to severely abuse their bodies as they confess their errors, to offer sacrifices and perform purifications, and to pray with quivering voices. For all these people, hope is fleeting.

tiles who had undergone the rite of circumcision) would have turned to the Lord. The proclamation of the gospel would then have extended to the Gentile population of the city, with perhaps many turning to the Lord right out of the various cults. Also at this time the gospel probably spread to the nearby city of Laodicea.

It is uncertain whether Paul ever visited the city himself. If he did, such a visit would have occurred during his lengthy stay at Ephesus. The apostle takes no credit for the establishment of the church in Colosse. Note 1:7, where he writes that they learned the gospel from Epaphras.

Among those who came to know Christ in the city is a man named Philemon. To him Paul writes a brief letter to intercede on behalf of his runaway slave Onesimus, who has encountered Paul in Rome and has come to know Christ (see 4:9; see commentary on Philemon).

These Christians gathered in homes for worship, teaching, and fellowship. There are at least two house churches that we know of—one in the home of a lady named Nympha (4:15), who lives in Laodicea, and the other in the home of Philemon (Philem. 2). There are probably a number of house fellowships in both of these cities. Nearly all believers throughout the Mediterranean world met in homes during the first century of the church's existence.

The Problem in the Church at Colosse

Paul writes this letter to counteract the inroads of a new and dangerous teaching in the church at Colosse. He denounces the teaching as empty, deceitful, and in accordance with elemental spirits (2:8).

What exactly are the contours of this teaching that the apostle finds objectionable? This question has been one of the most controversial issues surrounding the interpretation of this letter. The previous generation of scholarship thought the letter reflected the incursion of Gnosticism into the church.[9] This is unlikely because it is doubtful that Gnosticism as a religion of redemption yet existed at this early stage and the letter does not take on some of the key features of Gnosticism, such as the two-god theology.

In recent years, many scholars have suggested that the problem reflects a Jewish mysticism involving a visionary ascent to heaven and glimpses of angels surrounding the heavenly throne.[10] This view is more on the right track because there appears to be clear Jewish aspects to the teaching, such as the observance of Sabbaths and New Moon festivals (see 2:16). Yet this perspective does not explain all of the evidence, especially that which suggests the influence of local religions and religious practices. The Colossian problem is best described as a *syncretism*—a blending of religious ideas from a variety of local traditions.

A Portrait of the Situation

Word has reached the apostle Paul, perhaps through Epaphras, that trouble is brewing in the Colossian church. An influential leader—perhaps a shaman-like figure—is attracting a following among the believers. This spiritual guide claims superior insight into the spirit realm and is insisting on certain rites, taboos, and practices as a means of protection from evil spirits and for deliverance from afflictions and calamities. Paul characterizes his teaching as a "philosophy" (2:8).

One of the distinctive features of this teaching is "the worship of angels" for assistance and protection (2:18). This resonates well with the people who were accustomed to invoking spirit mediator beings in their pre-Christian lives. Although these people have received Christ as their Redeemer and Lord, they have not drawn out the full implications of this for their daily lives. Rather than relying directly on their powerful Lord, they invoke spirit assistants, or angels, to protect them from curses, to drive away spirits causing fevers, headaches, or horrible nighttime apparitions. Part of this probably involves the wearing of magical amulets, which normally bear the names of angels and spirits who they believe will provide protection.

The outspoken leader of the faction appears to be basing his unique spiritual insight, in part, on his prior experience of initiation into one or more of the local mystery cults. Paul alludes to this in 2:18 when he describes the deviant teaching using a rare word (*embateuō*) that is part of the technical vocabulary of a local cult. On the basis of his prior initiation, the shaman claims a certain immunity to the hostile powers and a superior understanding of the realm of gods and spirits.

In the teaching of this spiritualistic "philosophy," one must also observe a variety of taboos, such as fasting, avoidance of certain foods, and possibly also sexual regulations. In essence, there is such a rigor of discipline that Paul speaks of it as an unsparing or "harsh treatment of the body" (2:23).

Some other features of the teaching ultimately come from Judaism. Sabbath observance, festivals and New Moon celebrations, "humility" (probably referring to fasting), and "wisdom" all suggest Jewish roots. One must remember, however, that we should not always think of Judaism through the lenses of the Pharisees. There is clearly a dimension of what we may call "folk Judaism" in this countryside setting of western Asia Minor. In folk Judaism, there is a form of "wisdom" informing Jews about how to command and manipulate demons, especially by calling on angels.

After hearing about the spreading influence of this esoteric philosophy, Paul feels compelled to write to the Colossians and respond to this deviant teaching by pointing them to a proper perspective on the exalted Christ. In essence, he disqualifies the ringleaders of this teaching from leadership and urges the Colossians to desist from these practices, to cling to Christ, and to ignore their damning criticisms.

Introduction to the Letter (1:1–2)

Paul . . .and Timothy (1:1). The first line of the letter explicitly says that it is written not just by Paul, but also by Timothy, Paul's close companion. Paul's contribution far overshadows that of Timothy, especially when he switches to the first person ("I, Paul . . .") in 1:23 and writes autobiographically. Timothy is most likely functioning as Paul's secretary (a position the Greeks called an *amanuensis*).[11] In this role, Timothy may very well have had an active part in crafting the letter.

Grace and peace to you from God our Father (1:2). The standard convention in Greek letter-writing was to begin by pronouncing greetings (using the word *chairein*). Paul varies from this convention by using the word *charis* ("grace"). By this, he deepens the greeting by calling on the one true God to manifest his dynamic generosity upon these dear believers. He also adds to this the typical Jewish greeting of "peace" (Heb. *shalōm;* Gk. *eirēnē*). The peace of God is a key part of the eschatological blessings of the new covenant.

Thanksgiving and Prayer (1:3–14)

As almost all commentators concur, Paul shapes his thanksgiving and prayer to address the real situation of the readers. Paul feels a pastoral responsibility for this church because it was planted during his ministry in Ephesus by one of his converts. He genuinely prays for this group and gives thanks to God for them.

We always thank God when we pray (1:3). Paul often describes his prayer as unceasing. We can assume that at the minimum this means that he prays three times a day, as was common in Jewish practice. Beyond this, he probably finds many hours to pray for the many churches and people he cared for during his long days as an incarcerated prisoner. Apparently Timothy joins him for many extended times of prayer.

Love you have for all the saints (1:4). The emphasis on tangible manifestations of love is the distinctive trait that set Christianity apart from all of the other religions of the time. The self-sacrificial love of Christ is the benchmark for Paul's definition of love (see Eph. 5:1–2).

Hope that is stored up for you in heaven (1:5). To a people worried about life after death and the fate-determining stars in heaven, the notion that God is sovereign and is ultimately in control of their fate, granting them an eternal hope, is especially comforting. The threefold repetition of hope in the first chapter (1:5, 23, 27) may suggest that some of the Colossians still struggle with feelings of hopelessness.

Truth (1:5–6). In affirming that the Colossians have received a *true* gospel and that they now know the grace of God in *truth*, Paul anticipates his later comments about the *deceit* of the new teaching in the church (2:8) as well as the deceitfulness of the various idolatrous religions in the area.

All over the world this gospel is bearing fruit and growing (1:6). The gospel has literally spread into almost every reach of the Roman empire by the time Paul writes. The apostle is probably familiar with many incredible stories of the penetration of the gospel into places like Egypt, North Africa, and Persia.

You learned it from Epaphras (1:7). Here Paul credits this important Colossian leader as the first to bring these people the gospel. He not only evangelized the Lycus Valley cities, but the term "learned" implies that he continued to instruct them in the faith. Epaphras has just reported to Paul the good news about the spiritual vitality of the Colossian believers, but has also related the threat posed to the stability and well-being of the church by the faction that has developed.

That you may live a life worthy of the Lord (1:10). Literally, Paul writes, "that you *walk* worthily of the Lord." Walking is a metaphor for one's conduct, which he uses three other times in Colossians (2:6; 3:7; 4:5). Paul encourages conduct that honors the Lord and is appropriate for Christians. The metaphor is Jewish (see Ex. 18:20; Deut. 13:4–5) and was not commonly used by Greeks. The Hebrew term *halak* is the root of the rabbinic term *Halakah*, rules or statutes designed to guide the daily life of an individual (see comments on Eph. 4:1). Many of the Pharisaic regulations were written down in the second century A.D. in the Mishnah.

Being strengthened with all power according to his glorious might (1:11). Paul links four terms conveying the idea of divine power. God's awesome power is available to his people. Folks in the Greco-Roman world sought power for a variety of reasons—for protection from evils or to acquire wealth or influence. Here God's power is manifested to believers to enable them to have patience and endurance as they experience suffering, temptation, deceitful teachers, and various difficulties in this present evil age.

Who has qualified you to share in the inheritance of the saints in the . . . light (1:12). The image that stands behind the language of this verse is the anticipation of God's people as they wandered in the desert and waited to receive their inheritance in the Promised Land (see Num. 18:20; Deut. 10:19). The book of Daniel speaks of a future allotted inheritance (Dan. 12:13). The way Paul expresses himself here is similar to the way the Qumran community spoke of an eschatological inheritance: "God has caused them to inherit the lot of the Holy Ones. He has joined their assembly to the Sons of Heaven."[12] The difference, of course, is that Paul sees this fulfilled in the work of the Messiah, Jesus.

He has rescued us (1:13). The Exodus is once again the image that stands behind the words here. Paul compares God's deliverance of his people from their bondage in Egypt (Ex. 6:6; 14:30) to his mighty work now of rescuing believers from their bondage to the power of the evil one. Paul views his proclamation of the gospel as the means God uses for unbelievers "to open their eyes and turn them from darkness to light, and from the power of Satan" (Acts 26:18).

The dominion of darkness (1:13). The phrase refers to the sphere over which Satan and his demonic powers rule.

Brought us into the kingdom (1:13). The translation of the NIV does not bring out the color of the Greek verb Paul chooses here. *Methistēmi* was frequently used with the sense of transferal and often describes the massive dislocation of a group of one people from one region to another. The terminology may have reminded the Jewish readers of the time when the Syrian king Antiochus transferred several thousand Jews to Asia Minor in the second century B.C.[13] The believing community has not only been rescued from this evil domain, but they have been transplanted into a new dominion—the kingdom of God.

Redemption (1:14). Anyone in the Roman empire was readily familiar with this term because it commonly referred to the purchase of a slave. Readers who knew the Old Testament would rightly see an allusion here to God's freeing his people from their slavery in Egypt.[14] So much of the language of this passage points to a comparison between the first exodus from Egypt and now the second exodus of God's people from the more ultimate power of evil.

Poetic Praise to Christ (1:15–20)

This is one of the most beautiful and eloquent poems of praise to Christ in all of the New Testament. The piece magnificently celebrates Christ's sovereignty over all of creation and his supremacy over all powers, most notably the hostile angelic powers. Christ is truly Lord of heaven and earth.

The language and style of this passage have led many interpreters to regard the passage as a quotation of an actual hymn from the worship of the early church.[15] Colossians 3:16 intimates that this church regularly sang hymns of praise to Christ that were rich with statements about his identity and work. There is no doubt that this passage has many poetic features, but it is impossible for us to know with certainty that it is an actual hymn. If it were, it teaches us two important lessons: (1) The lyrics of the early Christian hymns were heavy with theological content, especially about Christ, and (2) Paul not only appeals to the intellect of his readers, but also to their hearts through the language of worship.

People in the Lycus Valley fear the influence of astral powers, terrestrial spirits, and underworld powers that raise problems for them in day-to-day life. This fear did not instantly go away for the Colossian believers after they turned to Christ. They know the reality of these powers and must still deal with them. The question for them is: What difference does Christ make? For the ringleader of the new teaching at Colosse, Christ is functionally no more powerful than the angels they invoke for protection. For Paul, Christ is the exalted Lord, Creator of the universe, preeminent in everything, and infinitely superior to any kind of angelic power.

He is the image of the invisible God (1:15). In the book of Proverbs, wisdom is personified and said to be with God at the creation of the world: "I was there when he set the heavens in place. . . . I was the craftsman at his side" (Prov. 8:27, 30). In the Jewish wisdom literature just before the New Testament era, this personified divine wisdom is described as the image of God: "For she is a reflection of eternal light, a spotless mirror of the working of God, and an image of his

◀

EARTH

goodness" (Wisd. Sol. 7:26). It was diffi-cult for Jewish Christians to reconcile the deity of Jesus Christ with their one-God theology (monotheism). Paul uses the language of wisdom to help clarify the nature and work of Christ in his exis-tence before his incarnation.

The firstborn over all creation (1:15). This expression does not mean that Christ is the first being God created. The Old Testament background is decisive here. This is a title that belongs to Christ as a descendant of David who reigns as king. The psalmist reports what God said of David: "I will also appoint him my *first-born*, the most exalted of the kings of the earth" (Ps. 89:27, italics added). The emphasis falls on Christ's ruling sover-eignty and the closeness of his relation-ship to the Father.

Whether thrones or powers or rulers or authorities (1:16). These terms were com-monly used in Jewish literature to speak of angelic powers, good or evil. Out of these sources, a passage in one first-cen-tury document uses three of the four terms: "I tell you, in all the creation which God created, there is not to be found one like you [Abraham]. For he searched among the angels and archangels, and principalities and powers, as well as thrones."[16] Although a hierarchy of angels may be assumed in Colossians 1:16, we have no way of discerning what that is. Although some have thought these are good angels, Paul consistently speaks of the "rulers" and "authorities" in a negative way in this letter (see 2:10, 15). By expanding on the invisible realm, Paul emphasizes to the Colossians that Christ is by no means an angel nor is he on the same level as an angel; he is Creator of this realm, and he is incomparably greater.

In him all things hold together (1:17). Christ not only brought all things into being, but he maintains the creation. J. B. Lightfoot once said that Christ is the One who makes creation "a cosmos instead of a chaos."[17] Not only does Christ keep the world from falling apart as a result of earthquakes, floods, plagues, and cosmic disturbances, he maintains a check on the awful workings of the demonic powers.

He is the head of the body, the church (1:18). Paul elaborates on his metaphor of the church as the body of Christ by now asserting that Christ functions as the head of this body. The image of a head in relationship to a body was common during Paul's time, especially in medical writers, some philosophers, and the Jew-ish writer Philo. Christ not only provides leadership and direction for his people, but he is the source of the church's life energy for its growth.[18]

God was pleased to have all his fullness dwell in him (1:19). The term "fullness" (*plērōma*) echoes the many places in the Old Testament where the essence, power, and glory of God inhabit the place he has chosen to dwell. The prophet Ezekiel exclaimed, "I looked and saw the glory of the LORD filling the temple" (Ezek. 44:4). This word may very well be another way of referring to the Holy Spirit, who dwelt in Jesus and empow-ered his ministry.

To reconcile to himself all things, whether things on earth or things in heaven (1:20). This passage holds out the promise of universal peace. The Messiah, as "Prince of Peace" (Isa. 9:6), will finally and ultimately bring worldwide peace and quell every upheaval and rebellion in all of creation. For the evil principalities and powers this means pacification as enemies of Christ, not a reconciliation to him as friends (see Col. 2:15).

Reconciliation (1:21–23)

Once . . . now (1:21–22). Paul elaborates on the nature of reconciliation by applying it particularly to the Gentile members of the Colossian church. In doing so he contrasts their former life ("once") with their present life in Christ ("now"). The "once–now" language appears frequently in early Christian literature to describe conversion.[19]

You were alienated from God and were enemies (1:21). Because they had given their devotion to idols such as Cybele, Apollo, and Aphrodite and lived in bondage to sinful practices, the Colossian Gentiles were estranged from the one true God.

To present you holy in his sight, without blemish and free from accusation (1:22). The aim of reconciliation goes beyond the enjoyment of a relationship with the living God. He wants to purify his people. The language of this verse comes from the context of sacrifice in Judaism. As an unblemished sacrificial animal was presented at the Jerusalem temple, so the Lord seeks to present his people to himself as pure. "Without blemish" was used to describe the animal offerings that the Lord required from his people and to characterize Christ in his self-sacrifice.[20] Paul shifts from the sacrificial language to a judicial image when he says "free from accusation." This was used in the common language of the day, as the papyri show, to refer to a person against whom no blame or fault could be brought.[21]

Not moved (1:23). Paul is deeply concerned that some of the Colossian believers are moving away from the core of the gospel. This is one of his principal reasons for writing the letter and the essential burden of Colossians 2.

Paul's Labor for the Gospel (1:24–29)

I fill up in my flesh what is still lacking in regard to Christ's afflictions (1:24). In Judaism and early Christianity, there was a conviction that a set amount of suffering must be endured by God's people before the final events of history are set in motion. This is clearly evident in Revelation 6:9–11, where the souls of the martyrs under the altar ask the Lord how much longer he will tarry before executing his work of judgment. They are told "to wait a little longer, until the number of their fellow servants and brothers who were to be killed . . . was completed." In a similar way, Jewish apocalyptic writers conceived of an appointed measure of suffering that must be fulfilled before the end of the age. One first-century Jewish writer puts it this way: "For [God] has weighed the age in the balance, and measured the times by measure, and

COLOSSE

Looking west from the top of the tel. ▼

numbered the times by number; and he will not move or arouse them until that measure is fulfilled" (*4 Ezra* 4:36–37).

What Paul clearly does not mean in this passage is that Christ's sufferings were in any way deficient for securing salvation for his people. Christ's sufferings are "still lacking" only in that they do not fill the appointed measure to usher in the end of the age. It appears that Paul saw his sufferings as contributing to the sum total that would hasten the coming of the Lord in judgment and final salvation.

By the commission God gave me (1:25). Paul here describes himself as an appointed steward in the unfolding of God's plan of salvation. The term *oikonomos* was widely used in Greco-Roman society for the work carried out by the administrator of a large household or an estate. In many contexts, the *oikonomos* was actually a slave.

The mystery (1:26–27). Paul is not referring here to the local religions that have mystery initiation rituals. He contrasts these with *the* mystery—the person of Christ. Jesus is the One who comes in fulfillment of the mystery spoken of in the book of Daniel (Dan. 2:18, 19, 27–30, 47), which is revealed to Nebuchadnezzar in a dream yet requires interpretation by divine insight. Jesus is the rock that was cut out "not by human hands," who has set up a kingdom that fills the whole earth and will never be destroyed (2:34–35, 44).

Christ in you, the hope of glory (1:27). As the core and essence of God's mystery, Christ indwells his people. He is directly and personally present in the lives of his people, who now constitute his body. This contrasts with Stoic notions of an impersonal and pantheistic immanence. Paul will build on this teaching in chapter 2 to raise the question of why they feel a need to call on angelic mediators when they are in a present and dynamic relationship with the risen Christ. The fact of Christ's presence also ensures them of a future life with him when he returns.

Admonishing and teaching everyone (1:28). Paul has invested enormous time and energy in teaching those who have come to Christ. This involved explaining the Old Testament in light of Jesus as the Messiah, passing on the teaching of and about Jesus, and explaining the kingdom of God. He has spent far more time teaching than simply an hour on Sunday morning and an hour on Wednesday evening. He has invested many hours of intensive sessions with small and large groups. Included with his teaching is direct and pointed criticism, admonition, and correction of the people. This would have been directed at engaging false beliefs as well as challenging these new believers to change their lifestyles.

Struggling with all his energy (1:29). In order to convey the significant effort involved in his ministry, Paul makes use of the athletic image of struggle (*agōn*). Paul's ministry on behalf of the church is comparable to the self-discipline and exertion of an athlete in training for competition. Yet Paul makes it clear that he does not depend only on his own strength, but on the supernatural enabling power that God bestows on him.

Paul's Labor for the Colossians (2:1–5)

In spite of his personal absence from the Colossians, Paul is deeply concerned about them and labors for them in prayer. For the first time, he mentions that he does not want them to be victimized to a teaching that is contrary to the gospel of Christ.

For those at Laodicea (2:1). Laodicea was only eleven miles down the Lycus River from Colosse. The church there was probably established at the same time as the church in Colosse by Epaphras (see 4:12–13; cf. 1:7). It is also addressed as one of the seven churches in the book of Revelation (Rev. 3:14–22), where it is called into account for its lukewarmness in the context of their material affluence and self-sufficiency.

Laodicea was in fact wealthy. Some of its leading citizens gained notoriety for their generous benefactions to the city. It was much larger than Colosse and served the area as a center for banking and finance. Much of the revenues for the city came from the production of textiles. The medical school of Laodicea, associated with the local deity Memn Karou, was also well known.[22]

For all who have not met me personally (2:1). Since Paul has never been to Colosse, only those who heard him preach the gospel in Ephesus would have had the opportunity to meet him personally. In spite of the fact that Paul did not plant this church, he has a deep and loving concern for their spiritual well-being. He labors in prayer for them, writes to them, and sends one of his trusted associates to minister to them.

Full riches of complete understanding (2:2). Paul wants to encourage the community and promote their unity in love, but this needs to be built on a foundation of proper knowledge. The word "com-plete" can more precisely be translated "full assurance" or "certainty." The writer of Hebrews uses this expression when he urges believers to "draw near to God with a sincere heart in *full assurance* of faith" (Heb. 10:22, italics added). This assurance is based on the forgiveness of sin and a knowledge of the Christian faith, to which he urges his readers to hold unswervingly (10:23).

In whom are hidden all the treasures of wisdom and knowledge (2:3). Christ, as the mystery of God, is the source of knowledge. Paul here draws on the personification of "wisdom" in the Old Testament (as well as in later Jewish literature) and transfers its functions to Christ:

> If you call out for insight
>   and cry aloud for understanding,
> and if you look for it as silver
>   and search for it as for hidden
>   treasure,
> then you will understand the fear of
>   the LORD
>   and find the knowledge of God.
> For the LORD gives wisdom,
>   and from his mouth come
>   knowledge and understanding.
>   (Prov. 2:3–6)

RUINS AT LAODICEA
▼

That no one may deceive you by fine-sounding arguments (2:4). Paul does not state this hypothetically. He is genuinely concerned that the Colossians are being deceived. In Greek writers such as Aristotle, Plato, and Epictetus, *pithanalogia* ("fine-sounding arguments") was not used with negative connotations, but with the sense of plausible and persuasive speech. The idea is similar to Paul's comments to the Corinthians that his preaching was "not with wise and persuasive words, but with a demonstration of the Spirit's power" (1 Cor. 2:4).

How orderly you are and how firm your faith in Christ is (2:5). Paul appeals to military imagery here, as he so often does in his letters (see Eph. 6:14–17), to convey the reality of the threat posed by the variant teaching. "Order" (*taxis*) is used in Greek literature and in the Old Testament for troops drawn up in battle formation. "Firm" (*stereōma*) was often used to designate the strength of troop units in resisting the enemy. In the LXX, it is used to describe God as a place of refuge against the enemy: "The LORD is my rock, my fortress and my deliverer" (Ps. 18:2; cf. 71:3). Once again, the strength and ability for Christians to stand strong is through Christ.

Live in Christ! Don't Fall Prey to Seductive Teaching (2:6–8)

Rooted and built up in him (2:7). Paul combines the images of a tree and a building here to describe the stability of the foundation believers have already received in Christ (see also 1 Cor. 3:9).

See to it that no one takes you captive (2:8). The apostle uses a rare and colorful word to speak of the danger facing the Colossian believers. Greek dictionaries, in fact, report only two other occurrences of the word *sylagogeō* in the language: In one instance it is used for stealing property and in the other for taking a captive.[23] One of the root words (*syla*) was commonly used to refer to booty or plunder that was seized from a cargo ship.

Hollow and deceptive philosophy (2:8). Paul is not condemning here the traditional Greek philosophies, such as Platonism, Epicureanism, or Stoicism. The language of this passage points to a faction within the church who spoke of their own set of teachings as "philosophy." This usage accords with the broad way the word *philosophia* was used in antiquity to refer to anything from occult traditions to the Jewish sects and to the traditional Greek philosophies. The fact that Paul characterizes the teaching of the factional group as "hollow and deceptive" underlines the danger and threat that he sees it posing to the church.

The basic principles of this world (2:8). "Basic principles" is a translation of the Greek word *stoicheia*. The term may indeed have the idea of the rudiments of science or an institution (such as the fundamental principles of religion), but it can also be a designation for spirit beings (as it is translated by the NRSV: "elemental spirits of the universe"). It is this latter sense that best fits the context here and in 2:20.[24]

Stoicheia is used for spirit beings in Persian religious texts, magical papyri, astrological texts, and some Jewish documents. The word thus represents still another term in Paul's reservoir of terminology to refer to the powers of darkness in Colossians, along with principalities, powers, authorities, and thrones. The basic point of

▶ *Stoicheia* in Jewish Occultism

This word features prominently in a Jewish occult document known as the *Testament of Solomon*. The original form of this document was probably composed in the first-century A.D. and may have originated in Asia Minor. An astrological portion of this work probably circulated independently as early as the first century B.C. It provides significant insight into the usage of the term:

Then I [Solomon] commanded another demon to appear before me. There came to me thirty-six heavenly bodies [*stoicheia*], their heads like formless dogs.... When I, Solomon, saw these things, I asked them, saying, "Well who are you?" All at once, with one voice, they said, "We are thirty-six heavenly bodies [*stoicheia*], the world rulers of the darkness of this age."

Paul's teaching here is that the dangerous teaching at Colosse has a demonic root. Although it is passed along as human tradition, it can ultimately be traced to the inspiration of demonic spirits.

Your Resources in Christ (2:9–15)

You have been given fullness in Christ (2:10). Not only does the power and authority of God belong to the resurrected Christ, but believers share in it by virtue of their incorporation into him. The Colossian believers do not need to fear the evil supernatural realm or rely on the teaching of "the philosophy." They have direct and immediate access to the power of God through Christ.

The head over every power and authority (2:10). Many of the Colossian believers continue to live in the daily fear of the workings of underworld spirits, terrestrial spirits, and astral spirits, as they have been accustomed to throughout their lives. Because of their union to Christ, however, they now share in his authority over the powers of darkness. The word "head" clearly indicates here the

sense of "authority over." This is in line with its usage in the Old Testament and other Jewish documents.[25]

In him you were also circumcised (2:11). In an unusual twist, Paul introduces his remarks on baptism by first speaking of it metaphorically as circumcision. He here draws on and adapts the Old Testament teaching about the "circumcision of the heart."[26] Even the Qumran community referred to circumcision metaphorically, illustrated by a passage in the Dead Sea Scrolls that speaks of circumcision of the foreskin of evil inclination and stiffness of neck.

In the putting off of the sinful nature (2:11). "Sinful nature" is the NIV's translation of *sarx* (flesh). For Paul, literal

REFLECTIONS

PART OF THE REASON THAT WE STUMBLE AND LOSE heart in the midst of our struggles is because we do not recognize and fully appreciate our position in Christ. Our knowledge about Christ and his work impacts how we live and see ourselves. Recognizing the meaning and implications of our relationship to Christ should have a profound impact on how we live day-to-day.

circumcision is no longer a necessary or valid practice for the new covenant people of God, but a spiritual circumcision is vitally essential. This is the removal of believers' solidarity with Adam, which Paul refers to as "the body of sin" in Romans 6:6. Christ removes the determining power of sin and death and, in its place, asserts his own lordship.

Buried with him in baptism and raised with him (2:12). Paul calls on the Colossian believers to remember the meaning of their baptism as an identification with the death and burial with Jesus. They are no longer identified with Adam, but with Christ and his victory over sin and its power. The idea of dying and rising with Christ is central to Paul's theology and receives its fullest expression in Romans 6:3–11.

The concept of co-resurrection receives a much stronger emphasis here and in Ephesians (see Eph. 2:4–6) than in Romans. By emphasizing the Colossians' participation in the resurrection of Christ, Paul demonstrates their share in his authority over the realm of demons and evil spirits. Christ alone is sufficient to protect them from the "powers." They no longer need to rely on their former means of control offered by occultism, nor do they need to rely on the solution presented by "the philosophy."

God made you alive with Christ (2:13). Some of the mystery cults claimed to offer an experience of rebirth and new life through ritual initiation. A papyrus document called the "Mithras Liturgy" (although probably not actually linked to Mithraism) purports to prescribe the proper rites and invocations for an initiate to become immortal, be reborn, be unified with the deity, and enter a new

life.[27] By contrast, Paul declares that new life is only found through union with the resurrected Christ.

Having cancelled the written code (2:14). Paul illustrates God's complete forgiveness of all the sins of believers by a colorful image derived from the world of business in the first century. The "written code" (*cheirographon*) was a note of indebtedness. The term is used many times in the papyri and is even well attested in Jewish literature. One Jewish document well illustrates how it was used: "'Let us find how we might be able to repay you.' Without delay, I would bring before them the note (*cheirographon*) and read it granting cancellation."[28]

Jesus has cancelled the note of indebtedness believers have with God. Consequently, all of the penalties God has threatened because humanity has defaulted in its obligations to him are declared null and void because of Christ's work on the cross. Paul creatively takes the image one step further by saying that Christ has taken the note away from us and nailed it to the cross.

Having disarmed the powers and authorities (2:15). The death and resurrection of Christ marked a decisive victory over the evil supernatural realm. They have

REFLECTIONS

WE DO NOT NEED TO BROOD OVER the past. We realistically experience a new life in Christ. The imagery of "the written code" nailed to the cross reminds us that every single transgression against our God has been completely forgiven on the basis of the work of Christ.

been deprived of any effective power against Christ himself or against those incorporated into him and appropriating his power. The Greek word translated "disarmed" is found in other literature simply in the sense of "strip off," as one removes clothing (see the use of this verb in 3:9 and the related noun in 2:11). The evil powers are not totally divested of their power. They continue to be hostile and active, but they are powerless against the Colossian Christians insofar as these believers recognize and appropriate their authority in Christ.

He made a public spectacle of them (2:15). The idea here is of a public exposure leading to disgrace. The verb used here (*deigmatizō*) is used of Joseph's plan to expose Mary's pregnancy and thus bring public shame on her (Matt. 1:19). An ancient historian cites a Cyprian law that mandates an adulteress to cut her hair and thus be subject to contempt by the community (Dio Chrysostom 47[64]3). The powers of darkness are exposed as weak and ineffective against God. Their efforts to put Christ to death and thereby ruin the redemptive plan of God (1 Cor. 2:6–8) were exposed as

futile in light of God's power in raising Jesus from the dead. Their plotting was unmasked as ineffective in light of God's wisdom, who used Jesus' death as the means of reconciling people to himself.

Triumphing over them by the cross (2:15). Paul takes the idea of public exposure one step further by adopting the vivid image of a Roman triumph. When a general led his army to victory in battle, the returning army would celebrate their conquest with a "triumphal procession" (*thriambeuō*). The successful general led a tumultuous procession marching through the streets of Rome, followed by his army singing hymns of victory and jubilantly reveling in their conquest. The defeated king with all of his surviving warriors together with the spoils of war were also paraded along as a spectacle for all to see.[29]

By analogy, God has put the principalities and powers on public display as defeated enemies through Christ's death and resurrection. The demonic rulers and evil spirits are led in the celebration as vanquished enemies. The Lord Jesus Christ is due all praise, honor, and glory as the victorious general. E. F. Scott aptly

---

▶ The Triumphal Procession of Aemilius Paulus

The first-century writer Plutarch tells the story of the parade led by the victorious general Aemelius Paulus. Depicted in this passage was the disheartened king Perseus along with all of his arms, riches, children, and attendants:

> He [Perseus] was followed by a company of friends and intimates whose faces were heavy with grief.... The whole army also carried sprays of lau-

rel, following the chariot of their general [Aemilius] by companies and divisions, and singing, some of them divers songs intermingled with jesting, as the ancient custom was, and others paeans of victory and hymns in praise of the achievements of Aemilius, who was gazed upon and admired by all, and envied by no one that was good.[A-2]

comments that the safety of the Colossian believer

was to be found in the conciliation of the friendly powers by means of offerings, sacred rites, spells, and talismans, so that they would protect him against the opposing demons . . . but Paul insists always that this protection is offered by Christ and that all else is useless. . . . We have a power on our side which can overcome everything that is against us.[30]

▶

MAGICAL AMULET

This is a Christian amulet depicting a rider slaying a demon. The reverse side has the inscription: "Guard from every evil him who carries this amulet."

Don't Be Victimized by the Variant Teaching (2:16–23)

Paul now takes up a direct and incisive criticism of many features of the variant teaching at Colosse. His basic complaint is that these heretics have lost their connection to Christ by replacing him with their syncretistic practices and calling on angels.

Do not let anyone judge you (2:16). A group of believers within the church at Colosse are, in fact, judging and demeaning others who do not subscribe to their teachings (see 2:18, 20). The language of this passage (esp. the Gk. pronoun *tis*, "a certain person"), may point to an influential teacher—perhaps a shaman like figure—who is ringleader of this emerging faction.

A religious festival, a New Moon celebration or a Sabbath day (2:16). These are distinctively Jewish observances found together repeatedly in the Old Testament

---

▶ The Combination of Jewish Observances with Pagan Cult Practices

The church father Hippolytus describes the teaching of a Christian leader named Elchasai, who lived at the end of the first century. Elchasai was not from Colosse, but his teaching is an example of how a Christian could mix Jewish, Christian, and pagan cult practices. Hippolytus quotes an important aspect of this teaching of Elchasai:

> There exist wicked stars of impiety . . . beware of the power of the days of the sovereignty of these stars, and engage not in the commencement of any undertaking during the ruling days of these. And baptize not man or woman during the days of the power of these stars, when the moon, (emerging) from among them, courses the sky, and travels along with them.

Beware of the very day up to that on which the moon passes out from these stars, and enter on every beginning of your works. But, moreover, honour the day of the Sabbath, since that day is one of those during which prevails (the power) of these stars. Take care, however, not to commence your works the third day from a Sabbath, since when three years of the reign of the emperor Trajan are again completed from the time that he subjected the Parthians to his own sway,—when, I say, three years have been completed, war rages between the impious angels of the northern constellations; and on this account all kingdoms of impiety are in a state of confusion.[A-3]

and ardently advocated by the proponents of the Colossian "philosophy."[31] There is evidence in Josephus and from inscriptions that Sabbath observance was important to the Jews of Asia Minor.[32] There is also testimony from the inscriptions that Jews in Asia Minor customarily observed the important Jewish festivals (such as Passover and Pentecost).[33]

The adherents of "the philosophy" are apparently not law-abiding Jews from the local synagogue. They are Christians (some of whom are ethnically Jewish) who are holding on to certain aspects of the Jewish law and yet combining it with local folk beliefs. It is even possible that they are giving these festivals and observances a new interpretation.

Religious festivals of various kinds were important in the local religions of Colosse. Also, the observance of the New Moon was integral to the performance of certain mystery initiation rituals. A popular deity in the region (also attested in the coins of Colosse) was the moon god Memn. The various phases of the moon were important to the worship of this god. Interestingly, another deity worshiped at Colosse was the goddess Selene. Her name, in fact, is the Greek word for the moon; she was closely associated with Artemis and Hekate. In popular belief these three goddesses were believed to protect their worshipers from hostile spirits.

A shadow of the things that were to come (2:17). The Jewish festivals and observances, as they were taught in the Old Testament, were essentially a foretaste of a future reality, realized now in the Lord Jesus Christ (see Heb. 10:1).

False humility (2:18). The word "false" is not in the Greek text, but it is inferred from the context. In Jewish texts, the word for "humility" could be used for fasting and may refer to that discipline here. In both Jewish and pagan circles, fasting is seen as important for driving off evil spirits. One Jewish text illustrates this well: "But a pure fast is what I created, with a pure heart and pure hands. It releases sin. It heals diseases. It casts out demons."[34] Fasting was also a precondition in many religious contexts for successful visionary experience (something we know was part of the Colossian "philosophy").

The worship of angels (2:18). This expression provides us with a significant insight into an important feature of the deviant teaching at Colosse. Although some have suggested that we need to interpret it in terms of the angels performing the worship, it makes better sense to view the angels as the object of the veneration. The group in Colosse is apparently calling on angels for assistance and protection from evil spirits. This was the way people commonly sought angels in the first century—in folk Judaism, in local folk belief, and later, even in segments of early Christianity.[35] It is doubtful that the group had splintered off from the church and were worshiping angels as they would worship God and Christ. Rather, the unique word for "worship" (*thrēskeia*) should be understood in the sense of "invoking" or "calling on."

[Don't] let anyone . . . disqualify you for the prize (2:18). The Greek word translated here (*katabrabeuō*) was used in the context of the games and reflected the decision of the judge (*brabeus*) against someone. An athlete who did not receive a favorable decision by the judge could be disqualified or deprived of the prize.

Paul hereby says that the people involved in this church faction have no right to set themselves up as judges over the Colossian believers. Rather, they should resist the insistence of these teachers to invoke angels and engage in ascetic practices, in spite of their visionary claims.

Such a person goes into great detail (2:18). This is a highly disputed translation of a Greek word that is rare in the language, but is vital to understanding the nature of the teaching of the Colossian "philosophy." The basic meaning of *embateuō* is "entering," which has led to the extended meanings of "entering into an investigation of something" or "entering into the possession of something." The great difficulty is that no explicit object for entering is given in the Greek text.

Our understanding of the religious usage of this word was enhanced significantly by the discovery of the Apollo temple at Claros, about thirty miles north of Ephesus. The interior walls of the temple preserve many Greek inscriptions of official delegations coming to consult the oracle. In the process of consultation, the delegations often went through the mystery initiation ritual associated with the cult. There were two stages to the ritual: (1) the reception of the mysteries (or the initiation), and (2) an entering (*embateuō*) of the innermost sanctuary of the temple for the consultation. *Embateuō* thus functions as a technical term to refer to the second and highest stage of the ritual initiation.[36]

This suggests that the leader and perhaps others in this "philosophy" have experienced some form of mystery initiation ritual into one of the local cults. This may have bolstered their claim to spiritual authority based on the knowledge and visionary experiences they presumably received.

About what he has seen (2:18). Visionary experience was a core feature of mys-

▸ Calling on Angels for Protection

There are many inscriptions from Asia Minor mentioning angels. Most of these are invocations to angels for protection, deliverance, or assistance. An inscribed amulet found near the city of Cyzicus illustrates this tendency:

Michael, Gabriel, Ouriel, Raphael, protect the one who wears this. Holy, holy, holy. PIPI RPSS. Angel, Araaph, flee O hated one. Solomon pursues you.[A-4]

Another inscription found on a tablet in Patras (Achaia) illustrates the same tendency in a way that highlights the connection to daily life:

O angels, protect the household and lives of John and Georgia . . . Sabaōth, Eloeein, Ariēl,

Gabriēl, Michaēl, Raphaēl, Thelchiēl, Sisiēl, Ouriēl, Raphaēl, Daniēl, Ouriēl, Boreēl, Iaō, Sabaōth, Chariēl . . . O power of these angels and characters, give victory and favor to John and Georgia and this household while they live.[A-5]

◄

AMULET INVOKING ANGELS

This amulet calls upon Michael, Raphael, Gabriel, and Ouriel.

▶ Finding the Right Angel to Thwart a Demon

The *Testament of Solomon* (see *"Sto-icheia* in Jewish Occultism" at 2:8) contains Jewish folk tradition on dealing with demons. One portion of the text ostensibly helps a person discern what demon is causing a particular ailment. The remedy typically involves calling on the appropriate angel who can thwart the evil workings of that demon. Here are a few examples:

- Then I, Solomon, summoned the first spirit and said to him, "Who are you?" He replied, "I am the first decan of the zodiac and I am called Ruax. I cause heads of men to suffer pain and I cause their temples to throb. Should I hear only, 'Michael, imprison Ruax,' I retreate immediately."

- The third said, "I am called Artosael. I do much damage to the eyes. Should I hear, 'Ouriel, imprison Artosael,' I retreat immediately."
- The fourth said, "I am called Oropel. I attack throats, result in sore throats and mucus. Should I hear, 'Raphael, imprison Oropel,' I retreat immediately."
- The eleventh said, "I am called Katanikotael. I unleash fights and feuds in homes. If anyone wishes to make peace, let him write on seven laurel leaves the names of those who thwart me: 'Angel, Eae, Ieo, Sabaoth, imprison Katanikotael,' and when he has soaked the laurel leaves in water, let him sprinkle his house with the water and I retreat immediately."[A-6]

tery initiation ritual. The first-century writer Pausanias reports that the underworld deities near the Meander River in western Asia Minor would send visions to all whom they wished to enter their inner sanctuaries in ritual initiation (Pausanias 32.13). The so-called "Mithras Liturgy" illustrates what the initiate might see (using the same verb for seeing that appears in this verse):

> You will *see* yourself being lifted up and ascending to the height, so that you seem to be in midair . . . you will *see* all immortal things. For in that day and hour you will *see* the divine order of the skies: the presiding gods rising into heaven, and others setting. Now the course of the *visible* gods will appear through the disk of god. . . . And you will *see* the gods staring intently at you and rushing at you

. . . but rather going about in their own order of affairs.[37]

He has lost connection with the Head (2:19). The great problem with all of these highly spiritualistic practices is that

◀

A CAPTIVE OF WAR

A colossal statue of a Phrygian captive used as a pier in Corinth.

these people have got their eyes off of Christ. They are not holding on tight to the Lord Jesus. In his place, they have inserted many kinds of observances and practices from Judaism and local folk belief that are not only unnecessary, but are animated by demonic spirits. Paul's use of the word "Head" in this passage stresses Jesus' role as leader of his church; he is the One they should be looking to for direction, guidance, strength, and protection.

You died with Christ to the basic principles of this world (2:20). The best understanding of the word *stoicheia* (trans. here as "basic principles" of the world) is as a reference to hostile spirit powers or demons (see comments on 2:8). The idea of dying to the influence of the powers is a natural extension of Paul's thought on the implications of being united with Christ (Rom. 6:3–11; see comments on Col. 2:12).

Paul thus presents a message of freedom. Identification with Christ's death necessarily implies immunity from demonic tyranny. It does not come automatically for believers; it must be appropriated by struggling with the unseen realm (see his exhortation in the following verses). If the Colossian Christians are immunized against the demonic realm, there is now no reason for them to be tempted to follow the regulations of "the philosophy," which, ironically, Paul claims were inspired by the spirit powers themselves.

Do not handle! Do not taste! Do not touch! (2:21). Paul here apparently quotes from his opponents. These commands represent the taboos that characterized the lifestyle teaching of this movement within the church. Paul does not specify exactly what they prohibit,

but it probably has to do with abstinence from various foods and drinks and may be understood in connection with fasting and "humility" (see comments on 2:18).

An appearance of wisdom (2:23). The kind of "wisdom" exhibited by the leaders of the faction is not traditional Jewish wisdom (of the type recorded in Proverbs, Ecclesiastes, Wisdom of Solomon, or Wisdom of Jesus ben Sirach), nor is it a traditional Greek form of wisdom as represented by the philosophers. This was esoteric wisdom for dealing with spiritual powers. There was a strong tradition within folk Judaism of a wisdom for handling evil spirits that purportedly went back to Solomon. This tradition of Solomon's great wisdom for dealing with evil spirits is best illustrated by Josephus:

> Now so great was the prudence and *wisdom* which God granted Solomon that he surpassed the ancients, and even the Egyptians, who are said to excel all men in understanding, were not only, when compared with him, a little inferior but proved to fall far short of the king in sagacity.... There was no form of nature with which he was not acquainted or which he passed over without examining, but he studied them all philosophically and revealed the most complete knowledge of their several properties. And God granted him knowledge of the art used against demons for the benefit and healing of men. He also composed incantations by which illnesses are relieved, and left behind forms of exorcisms with which those possessed by demons drive them out, never to return. And this kind of cure is of very great power among us

> ▶ **Prohibitions in a Jewish Magical Text**

In Jewish folk belief, someone seeking a visionary experience typically needed to adhere to certain taboos and purity regulations. The *Sepher Ha-Razim* (*Book of Mysteries*), a collection of incantation texts from popular Judaism that invoked angels, cautions a careful observance of all the necessary taboos to elicit an appearance of the god Helios: "Guard yourself, take care, and keep pure for seven days from all impure food, from all impure drink, and from every unclean thing. Then on the seventh day . . . invoke seven times the names of the angels that lead him during the day."[A-7]

to this day, for I have seen a certain Eleazar, a countryman of mine, in the presence of Vespasian, his sons, tribunes and a number of other soldiers, free men possessed by demons, and this was the manner of the cure. . . . And when this was done, the understanding and *wisdom* of Solomon were clearly revealed.[38]

Harsh treatment of the body (2:23). This refers to the ascetic practices associated with the teaching of "the philosophy"— including fasting, various taboos, and other regulations. It is doubtful, though not impossible, that this included the self-flagellation and self-mutilation that characterized the local cult of Attis.

Seek the Things Above (3:1–4)

Based on their participation in the death and resurrection of Christ, believers partake of a new life. Here there is security, freedom of fear, and power for dealing with the influences of hostile powers.

Set your hearts on things above (3:1). The language and thought here are reminiscent of Jesus' exhortation to "seek first his kingdom" (Matt. 6:33). When Paul speaks of the "above," he is not so much thinking literally as spiritually. He has in mind all that characterizes "the age to come," life in the new covenant, and citizenship in heaven (see Phil. 3:20).

The right hand of God (3:2). There is an echo here of the language of Psalm 110:1: "The LORD says to my Lord: 'Sit at my right hand until I make your enemies a footstool for your feet.'" This passage was understood by Paul and the early Christians to be a messianic promise that God's Anointed One would be exalted to a position of prominence and authority after he defeated his enemies. Paul calls on Christians to meditate on the fact that they live in a vital connection to a sovereign Lord who has defeated his supernatural enemies—the same enemies they now face—and now sits enthroned in a position of preeminent authority.

Your life is now hidden with Christ in God (3:3). Paul stresses that the position of believers in Christ is a place of security. He employs the language of Isaiah and the Psalms to express the security of God's people as they trust in him when they face their enemies. In Psalm 27:5–6, the psalmist says, "For in the day of trouble he will keep me safe in his dwelling; he will hide me in the shelter of his tabernacle and set me high upon a rock." Isaiah 49:2 says, "In the shadow of his hand he hid me; he made me into a polished arrow and concealed me in his quiver" (see also Ps. 31:19–20).

Put Away the Sins of the Past (3:5–11)

Put to death, therefore, whatever belongs to your earthly nature (3:5). Using common physiological terminology, Paul creates a metaphor to describe the process of developing moral purity. Every believer needs to kill off the body parts that lead to sin. The language is reminiscent of Jesus' own teaching when he said, "If your right eye causes you to sin, gouge it out and throw it away" (Matt. 5:29).

Sexual immorality (3:5). Lists of vices were common in the moral exhortation of ancient writers, especially among the Stoics. Paul lists five items for the Colossians to work on, all of which have to do with sexual purity. This is not surprising given the sexual promiscuity of the time. *Porneia* is a broad term referring to every kind of sexual encounter outside of the bond of marriage.

REFLECTIONS

SINS OF DESIRE ARE PART OF THE past life that God wants us to bring under control. Greed involves constantly acquiring new "toys," spending large amounts of our money on entertainment and nonessentials, and planning our lives around the acquisition of wealth. A greedy spirit is ignored by mislabeling desires as needs.

Greed, which is idolatry (3:5). Greed applies to sex because it involves an insatiable appetite. Paul may not be limiting this word strictly to matters of sexuality here. In a cultural context rampant with idolatry, it is somewhat surprising to find Paul referring to greed as idolatry. In Paul's mind, however, anything (including unbridled sexual pleasures) that usurps the proper place of God in one's devotion is idolatry (see comments on Eph. 5:5).

The wrath of God is coming (3:6). Everyone will be called to accountability in the future about their misappropriation of God's gift of sexuality, as well as every other form of idolatry. This period of God's judgment is customarily called "the day of the LORD" in the Old Testament prophets. The prophet Zephaniah warns, "The great day of the LORD is near. . . . That day will be a day of wrath, a day of distress" (Zeph. 1:14–15; see also 1 Thess. 5:1–3).

Anger (3:8). Paul now addresses another group of five vices that focus on the nature of personal interaction among fellow believers. "Anger, rage, malice, slander, and filthy language" are destructive to the unity that should characterize the church and inconsistent with the kind of love that Christ models.

Since you have taken off your old self . . . and put on the new (3:9–10). The image of taking off and putting on clothing was widespread in the ancient world. The Old Testament speaks frequently of being clothed with strength, righteousness, and salvation, but there is never any mention of the removal of a sinful and corrupt nature.[39] Paul now gives the Colossians a better understanding of how a virtuous life is possible by speaking of conversion as a decisive supernatural event that reaches to the core of one's being.

The "old self" (one's identity in solidarity with the sin of Adam) has been removed and a "new self" (one's identity in union with Christ) has replaced it. This change of identity serves as the basis of dealing with vice and appropriating virtue. There is thus also a sense in which believers now need to actualize what has already taken place spiritually—they need to take off the old self and put on the new self (see also comments on Eph. 4:22–24).

Barbarian (3:11). Among the Greeks and Romans, "barbarians" were people who lacked the civility of Greek or Roman culture. A barbarian could be any foreigner who spoke a language other than Greek or Latin and was different in appearance, manners, and behavior.[40]

Scythian (3:11). Historically, the Scythians were northern people located along the northern coast of the Black Sea in the area of what is today southern Ukraine. To the Greeks, the Scythians were a violent, uneducated, and uncivilized people. Josephus reflects a common view of the Scythians when he says, "Now, as to the Scythians, they take a pleasure in killing men, and differ little from brute beasts."[41] For those who have been incorporated into the body of Christ, there is no longer a distinction between people based on ethnicity, culture, gender, or social status.

Put On the Virtues of Christ (3:12–17)

Paul calls on the Colossian believers to cultivate a variety of Christian virtues that are essential for life in their new community. He carefully weaves into his admonitions the reasons why they are now able to change their attitudes, lifestyle, and behavior. Not only have they participated in Christ's death and resurrection and received a new self, but they are also chosen by God and have received purity, love, forgiveness, peace, and the word of Christ.

Bear with each other (3:13). This needs to be tempered by what Paul has said in Colossians 2. The false teaching should not be patiently endured. Yet if the leaders of the faction turn away from their teaching in accordance with Paul's instructions, the Colossians should be quick to forgive and embrace them in love.

Let the peace of Christ rule in your hearts (3:15). "Rule" does not capture the full significance of the word *brabeuō* (see comments on 2:18). This is a metaphor that comes from the context of athletic games where an official would serve as an umpire in judging a conflict. The Colossians are not only living in fear of the realm of the demonic, but they are now in turmoil because of the teaching of "the philosophy," not to mention all of the other concerns of day-to-day life. These internal fears and storms should be adjudicated by the wonderful gift of peace from the Messiah (see also John 14:27; Phil. 4:6).

The word of Christ (3:16). At this early time, it is doubtful that the Colossians possess any of the four Gospels, yet they have plenty of teaching about Jesus. They have received this from the oral tradition stemming from Palestine that was passed on to them from Paul via Epaphras. As we have already mentioned, part of this may have been hymns that were rich in teaching about Jesus (as 1:15–20 may have been). Paul here encourages them to continue meditating on the teaching about Christ, especially as it is imparted to them in their hymns of praise to Christ.

Psalms, hymns and spiritual songs (3:16). This expression describes the full range of forms in use in the Colossian church. It is possible that "psalms" represents more of a Jewish style and "hymns" a Greek form. Both terms, however, are used in the book of Psalms. The word "spiritual" goes with all three and characterizes the work of the Holy Spirit in moving Christians to write lyrics and songs in praise of Jesus in the early church (see comments on Eph. 5:19).

Proper Behavior in the Christian Household (3:18–4:1)

This is the earliest example of a set of instructions to the various members of a Christian household (see "Household Duties" at 1 Peter 2:11). There are many examples of these kinds of instructions in antiquity, both in Hellenistic Judaism and in Hellenistic popular philosophy (such as Stoicism). One of the key distinguishing features of this household code from non-Christian codes is the new basis and motivation. Seven times in these eight verses Paul roots his instructions "in the Lord." It is crucial to recognize that Paul is not admonishing these believers to conform to the prevailing cultural patterns, but rather to evaluate everything they do in light of the teaching about Jesus and the pattern he left for his people to emulate.

Wives, submit to your husbands, as is fitting in the Lord (3:18). Paul urges wives to recognize that there is an order of authority in the Christian household. There was a strong cultural patriarchy in the homes of antiquity. The first-century writer Plutarch comments, "If they [the

▸ Obeying and Honoring Parents in a Jewish Home

Philo, a first-century Jew living in Alexandria, Egypt, writes about the obligation of children in the home to honor their parents.

> Parents have not only been given the right of exercising authority over their children, but the power of a master.... For parents pay out a sum many times the value of a slave on their children. They also invest in nurses, tutors and teachers, in addition to the cost of their clothes, food and care in sickness and health from their earliest years until they are full grown.
>
> Given all these considerations, children who honor their parents do nothing deserving of praise since even one of the items mentioned is in itself quite a sufficient call to show deep respect. And on the contrary, they deserve blame, a sharp reprimand, and extreme punishment who do not respect them as seniors nor listen to them as instructors nor feel the duty of repaying them as benefactors nor obey them as rulers nor fear them as masters.
>
> Therefore, honor your father and mother next to God, he [Moses] says [Ex. 20:12].... For parents have little thought for their own personal interests and find their fulfillment and happiness in the high excellence of their children, and to gain this the children will be willing to listen to their instructions and to obey them in everything that is just and profitable; for the true father will give no instruction to his son that is foreign to virtue.[A-8]

wives] subordinate themselves to their husbands, they are commended, but if they want to have control, they cut a sorrier figure than the subjects of their control."[42] Another writer states the role of wives quite simply: "For it is proper for a wife to be subject to her husband."[43]

In a Roman household, the eldest male was in authority as the *paterfamilias*. What is vitally significant here is that Paul qualifies the submission by "as is fitting in the Lord." Once again, culture is not the guide, but God's revelation on issues of role relationships and order. In Ephesians 5, Paul bases this order in the marriage relationship on the pattern of Christ's relationship to the church.

Husbands, love your wives and do not be harsh with them (3:19). Christian husbands are to avoid being insensitive and overbearing with their wives. This contrasts significantly to many Roman households. Plutarch speaks of Roman men who "rage bitterly against their wives."[44] Paul goes one step further by enjoining men to love their wives—with the kind of love modeled to us by the Lord Jesus (see 3:12, 14; Eph. 5:25).

Children, obey your parents in everything (3:20). The fifth commandment instructs children to "honor" their parents (Ex. 20:12). In a Jewish context where children were still minors, honor was demonstrated by obedience.

Fathers, do not embitter your children (3:21). Because of their position in the household, fathers may be tempted to be severe with their children. Paul advises restraint for the practical reason of not overly discouraging the children. Even Roman writers at times admonished fathers to exercise restraint and sensitiv-

ity. Plutarch advises, "I do not think they [fathers] should be utterly harsh and austere in their nature, but they should in many cases concede some shortcomings to the younger person, and remind themselves that they once were young."[45]

Slaves, obey your earthly masters (3:22). The very presence of this admonition reminds the modern reader that the small church at Colosse consisted of both slave owners and slaves. Philemon is probably one of these slave owners (see Philemon). Although Paul may have objected to the institution of slavery, he advises Christians on how to live within the parameters of this thoroughly entrenched economic and social structure. He urges slaves to obey their masters. He pens these remarks at a time when he has recently come in contact with the disobedient slave, Onesimus, who fled Colosse and his master, Philemon. One must always remember to sharply distinguish the features of slavery in the Roman era from slavery in the ante-bellum South (see comments on slavery in the commentary on Philemon and at Eph. 6:5–9).

Working for the Lord (3:23). Slaves could potentially lack motivation for their work and engage in their responsibilities with an attitude of drudgery. Paul prescribes a new motivation. Ultimately they serve a different master, and it is him that they should seek to please.

Anyone who does wrong will be repaid for his wrong (3:25). This would encourage slaves who had been unfairly treated by their masters. There is a time of judgment for the recompense of every injustice. This was also a warning for the slaves to conduct their service with integrity.[46]

Masters, provide your slaves with what is right and fair (4:1). Paul now appeals to the slave owners not only to respond to their slaves with a sense of justice, but also to treat them with "equality" (*isotēs*). Paul clearly sows the seeds for the eventual dismantling of this unjust social structure.

The Roman writer Seneca also advocated treating slaves with justice: "Be moderate in what you tell slaves to do. Even with slaves, one ought to consider not how much you can make them suffer without fearing revenge, but how much justice and goodness allow" (Seneca, *On Mercy* 1.18).[47] Notably absent from Seneca, however, is any reference to treating slaves with "equality." In the Christian community, slaves are "no longer a possession subject to their master's caprice, but brothers in Christ."[48] A Jewish group called the Essenes denounced slavery as an outrage to the principle of "equality" (*isotēs*).[49]

Final Instructions (4:2–6)

Devote yourselves to prayer (4:2). Paul urges the Colossian believers to maintain a constant attitude of prayer. This continuance in prayer probably includes but goes well beyond maintaining a schedule of set times to pray during the day. In Judaism, it was typical to pray three times a day—at morning, noon, and night. The word for "devote" (*proskartereō*) is used in Mark 3:9 to describe a boat that was being kept ready for Jesus. Prayer is especially vital at this juncture for the Colossians as the means of staying in close contact with the Head of the church, who can give them counsel, guidance, and strength regarding their threatening situation.

Being watchful (4:2). This expression echoes the teaching of Jesus. The Lord admonished his disciples to "watch and pray" so that they would not fall into temptation (Mark 14:38). This is wise counsel to the Colossian believers who are tempted to follow the teachings of "the philosophy."

That God may open a door for our message (4:3). The image of an "open door" to represent an opportunity for some activity was widely used in the ancient world. The Stoic writer Epictetus uses the image in the sense of, "I am free to go anywhere."[50] Paul uses the image elsewhere to speak of an opportunity for the presentation of the gospel (1 Cor. 16:9; 2 Cor. 2:12). He can only rely on God to provide opportunities, since his freedom is being severely restricted by imprisonment.

I am in chains (4:3). The reference to "chains" reminds the Colossians that Paul is in Roman custody, awaiting trial. He has been imprisoned for up to three years now (two years in Caesarea and for up to a year in Rome). Most likely Paul is literally in shackles of some sort. A Roman jurist once advised, "If the officer in charge of a prison is bribed to keep someone in custody without chains . . . he must be punished by the court."[51]

Be wise in the way you act toward outsiders (4:5). "Outsiders" is a Jewish manner of expression for those who are outside of the community of the covenant people of God. Here it refers to unbelievers in the city of Colosse and the surrounding countryside. Paul urges the Colossian believers to exercise God-given wisdom in their interactions with people they encounter at the marketplace, at work, and at civic functions. These new believers would be under scrutiny by people wondering why they have left the synagogue or have forsaken their allegiance to the local cults.

Seasoned with salt (4:6). Job asks rhetorically, "Is tasteless food eaten without salt?" (Job 6:6). Everyone in the ancient world used salt to season their food. A discussion "seasoned with salt" became a way of referring to an interesting, stimulating, and enjoyable conversation or discourse. One ancient writer bemoaned the presentations of certain philosophers as "unsalted."[52]

Whenever the Colossian Christians have opportunity to interact with unbelievers, Paul wants them to engage in lively and interesting conversation. The image that he provides us of the Colossian church is not of a group who have disengaged from the world and are huddling together in isolation. His comments presuppose a group of people involved in the community and bearing a vibrant testimony.

Personal Greetings and Instructions (4:7–18). Paul extends greetings to the Colossians from eight coworkers currently serving with him in Rome.

Tychicus (4:7). A trusted colleague of Paul's originally hailing from Asia Minor (see Acts 20:4) and possibly known by the Colossians, Tychicus will carry the letter and share further details with them personally (see comments on Eph. 6:21).

Onesimus (4:9). This is Philemon's fugitive slave (see Philem. 10). Somehow this runaway slave has encountered Paul, become a Christian, and ministered to the apostle faithfully in his imprisonment. It is striking that Paul can commend him to the Colossian congregation

as a "dear brother." Colosse was the hometown of Onesimus.

My fellow prisoner Aristarchus (4:10). Paul is not the only believer imprisoned in Rome. His companion Aristarchus shares the same plight. Although we do not know the circumstances of this man's imprisonment, presumably it stems from his bold proclamation of the gospel (Acts 20:4). Aristarchus, a Jewish Christian, was part of the fruit of Paul's ministry at Thessalonica. He subsequently joined Paul for at least a part of his work at Ephesus, where he was a victim in the mob

HIERAPOLIS

Hillside pools in terraces formed by lime deposits from calcareous spring water.

scene at the theater (19:29). He accompanied Paul on his return journey through Macedonia, Greece, Troas, Miletus, and on to Jerusalem, where Paul was arrested. Aristarchus was also with Paul on the harrowing sea journey from Caesarea to Rome (27:2).

Mark, the cousin of Barnabas (4:10). This is none other than John Mark from Jerusalem, the cousin of Barnabas and the son of Mary, who hosted a church in her home (Acts 12:12). In an amazing display of reconciliation, Paul has apparently been reunited with this young man after he defected during Paul's first missionary journey (12:12; 13:13). Paul's concern about Mark's suitability for further apostolic activity had been so strong that he refused to take him along on the second journey. This resulted in Paul and Barnabas going separate ways (15:36–40).

Now, however, Mark is with Paul in Rome as the apostle's "fellow worker" (Philem. 24). Mark is well known in church history for subsequently becoming the apostle Peter's companion (1 Peter 5:13) and for writing the second Gospel, based on Peter's preaching.[53]

Jesus, who is called Justus (4:11). This is the only time this coworker of Paul's is mentioned in Scripture, and we know nothing else about him from other sources. His Jewish name was actually quite common and is also rendered in English as "Joshua." As with many other Jews in the Greco-Roman era (such as Saul-Paul), he took on a Hellenistic Roman name.

He is always wrestling in prayer for you (4:12). Paul commends his fellow worker, Ephaphras, for his diligence in praying for the Colossians. Once again, Paul appropriates an image from an athletic competition to describe the intense effort and struggle that Epaphras gives to prayer (see comments on 1:29).

Luke, the doctor (4:14). Luke was the traveling companion of Paul and the author of the Gospel bearing his name and the book of Acts (25 percent of the New Testament). The combined efforts of Paul and Luke account for half the New Testament. This is the only reference to Luke as a doctor. We know nothing about the nature of his medical training or his practice prior to joining Paul.

Demas (4:14). In a tragic turn of events a few years later, Demas takes a serious fall. Paul writes in his letter to Timothy: "Demas, because he loved this world, has deserted me" (2 Tim. 4:10).

Nympha and the church in her house (4:15). This verse reminds us that the early church met exclusively in homes, which continued to be the case for the next two hundred years. Nympha was apparently a wealthy Laodicean woman who became a Christian and opened her home as a meeting place for one of the Laodicean house groups. She may be singled out here for greeting because Paul,

REFLECTIONS

A HYMN WRITER ONCE SPOKE OF a time of prayer as "a sweet hour of prayer." Indeed, communion and fellowship with our Lord is sweet and enjoyable. Yet intercessory prayer is normally strenuous. It requires a commitment of time, mental energy, discipline, and passion.

Timothy, or one or more of the associates knows her personally.

You in turn read the letter from Laodicea (4:16). In addition to this letter, Paul has apparently written another letter to the church at Laodicea, which Tychicus delivers. Unfortunately, this letter has not been preserved. Despite much speculation, it is not to be identified with Paul's letter to the Ephesians or with the fourth-century apocryphal *Letter to the Laodiceans*.[54] This passage underlines the close association between the churches of Laodicea and Colosse. It also illustrates the fact that Paul's letters were read aloud to the churches when they were received. This most certainly must have been followed by extended times of interaction, questions, and dialogue.

Archippus (4:17). He is only mentioned here and in Philemon 2 in the entire New Testament. Paul speaks of him in Philemon as a "fellow soldier" and as a member of Philemon's Colossian house church. We have no way of knowing what special ministry Paul calls him to complete.

I, Paul, write this greeting in my own hand (4:18). Paul concludes his letter by taking the stylus and signing it personally (see also 1 Cor. 16:21; 2 Thess. 3:17). It is likely that Timothy had been composing the letter as his *amanuensis* (or secretary).

ANNOTATED BIBLIOGRAPHY

Arnold, Clinton E. *The Colossian Syncretism: The Interface Between Christianity and Folk Belief at Colosse.* Grand Rapids: Baker, 1996 (orig. pub. as WUNT 2/77 [Tübingen: J. C. B. Mohr, 1995]).

This is a detailed background study on Colossians. In it I contend that the "Colossian heresy" can be best understood as a local syncretistic folk belief that has at its root a fear of hostile powers resolved in part by calling on angels for protection, help, and assistance.

Barth, Markus and Hemut Blanke. *Colossians.* AB 34B. Garden City, N.Y.: Doubleday, 1995.

This is the most detailed and extensive commentary on Colossians currently available. There is much historical information available here.

Bruce, F. F. *The Epistles to the Colossians, to Philemon, and to the Ephesians.* NICNT. Grand Rapids: Eerdmans, 1984.

This is a well-written and informative commentary.

Dunn, James D. G. *The Epistles to the Colossians and to Philemon.* NIGTC. Grand Rapids: Eerdmans, 1996.

One of the strengths of this work is Dunn's ability to draw out the relevant Jewish background to the terms and theological concepts.

Garland, David. *Colossians and Philemon.* NIVAC. Grand Rapids: Zondervan, 1998.

This commentary is a blend of good interpretive insight with relevant application.

Lightfoot, J. B. *St. Paul's Epistles to the Colossians and to Philemon.* Grand Rapids: Zondervan, 1977 (orig. pub. 1879).

Lightfoot's commentary is still of great value for its many insights. Few have matched Lightfoot's knowledge of the ancient sources and his ability to bring them to bear on the text of the New Testament.

O'Brien, Peter T. *Colossians, Philemon.* WBC 44. Waco, Tex.: Word, 1982.

This served for many years as the best exegetical commentary on Colossians.

Main Text Notes

1. For more information about the city of Colosse, see C. E. Arnold, "Colosse," *ABD*, 1:1089–90.

2. Cicero, *Flac.* 28.68.

3. Tacitus, *Ann.* 14.27; Eusebius, *Chronica* 1.210.

4. See W. H. Mare, "Archaeological Prospects at Colosse," *NEASB* 7 (1976): 39–59. Professor Daria de Barnardi Ferrero, director of the Italian group currently excavating Hierapolis, clarified for me by letter that she is not aware of any group that has recently gained permission to excavate the site.

5. The coins have been published (with photographs) by Hans von Aulock, *Münzen und Städte Phrygiens* (Part 2; Istanbuler Mitteilungen, Beiheft 27; Tübingen: Ernst Wasmuth, 1987), 24–27, 83–93 (nos. 443–595).

6. Many of these have now been published with an English translation and discussion by J. G. Gager, *Curse Tablets and Binding Spells from the Ancient World* (New York/Oxford: Oxford Univ. Press, 1992).

7. See ch. 3 ("The Local Veneration of Angels") in C. E. Arnold, *The Colossian Sycretism* (Grand Rapids: Baker, 1996), 61–89.

8. On the cult of Cybele, see M. J. Vermaseren, *Cybele and Attis* (London: Thames and Hudson, 1977).

9. This view is advocated, e.g., by William Barclay, *The Letters to the Philippians, Colossians, and Thessalonians* (Daily Study Bible; rev. ed.; Louisville: Westminster, 1975).

10. See, e.g., the commentaries by F. F. Bruce (*The Epistles to the Colossians, to Philemon, and to the Ephesians* [NICNT; Grand Rapids: Eerdmans, 1984], 17–26) and P. T. O'Brien (*Colossians, Philemon* [WBC 44; Waco, Tex.: Word, 1982], xxx–xxxviii).

11. See H. Y. Gamble, "Amanuensis," *ABD*, 1:172. An entire book has now been devoted to this theme; see E. R. Richards, *The Secretary in the Letters of Paul* (WUNT 2/42; Tübingen: J. C. B. Mohr, 1991).

12. 1QS 11:7–8.

13. Josephus, *Ant.* 12.3.4 §149.

14. See Ex. 6:6; 13:15; 15:13; Isa. 51:10.

15. There is more written about this passage in Colossians than any other. For a recent and detailed discussion about the passage as a hymn, see M. Barth and H. Blanke, *Colossians* (AB 34B; New York: Doubleday, 1994), 227–46.

16. *T. Ab.* 13:10.

17. J. B. Lightfoot, *Saint Paul's Epistles to the Colossians and to Philemon* (Grand Rapids: Zondervan, 1977; originally printed in 1879), 156.

18. See C. E. Arnold, "Jesus Christ: 'Head' of the Church," in *Jesus of Nazareth: Lord and Christ*, eds. M. M. B. Turner and J. B. Green (Grand Rapids: Eerdmans, 1994), 346–66.

19. See Rom. 11:30–31; Gal. 4:8–9; Eph. 2:2–3, 11–13; 1 Peter 2:10.

20. See Lev. 22:21; Num. 19:2; Heb. 9:14; 1 Peter 1:19.

21. Walter Grundmann, "ἀνέγκλητος," *TDNT*, 1:356–57.

22. For more information on Laodicea, see F. F. Bruce, "Laodicea," *ABD*, 4:229–31.

23. See MM, 596.

24. For a detailed discussion and a listing of the primary-source evidence, see my *Colossian Syncretism*, 158–94.

25. See Deut. 28:13; Judg. 10:18; 11:8, 9; Philo: *Creation* 119; *Flight* 110, 182; *Dreams* 2.207; *Life of Moses* 2.30, 82; *Special Laws* 3.184; *Questions on Genesis* 1.3, 10; 2.5; *Questions on Exodus* 2.124.

26. See Lev. 26:41; Deut. 10:16; Jer. 4:4; Ezek. 44:7, 9.

27. The text is found in the Great Paris Magical Papyrus, *PGM* 4.475–829.

28. *T. Job* 11:11.

29. For additional detailed discussion on this and the previous two images, see my *Colossian Syncretism*, 277–87. See also L. Williamson, "Led in Triumph: Paul's Use of Thriambeuo," *Int* 22 (1968): 317–32.

30. E. F. Scott, *Epistles to the Colossians, to Philemon, and to the Ephesians* (London: Hodder & Stoughton, 1936), 50.

31. See 1 Chron. 23:31; 2 Chron. 2:4; 31:3; Ezek. 45:17; Hos. 2:11.

32. For references, see Paul Trebilco, *Jewish Communities in Asia Minor* (SNTSMS 69; Cambridge: Cambridge Univ. Press, 1991), 17–18, 198–99.

33. Ibid., 199, note 70.

34. *Apoc. Elijah* 1:20–21.

35. See Part I: "The Worship of Angels," in my *Colossian Syncretism*, 8–102.

36. For the texts, translation, and a detailed discussion of these inscriptions, see ch. 5 in my *Colossian Syncretism*, 104–57.

37. *PGM* 4.539–85.

38. Josephus, *Ant.* 8.2.5 §§ 41–49.

39. See 2 Chron. 6:41; Ps. 132:9; Isa. 51:9; 52:1.

40. See Thomas E. J. Wiedemann, "Barbarian," in *OCD*³, 233.

41. Josephus, *Ag. Ap.* 2.38 §269; see Karen S. Rubinson, "Scythians," in *ABD*, 5:1056–57.

42. Plutarch, *Conjugalia praecepta* 33.

43. Both texts are cited from E. F. Lohse, *Colossians and Philemon* (Hermenia; Philadelphia, Fortress, 1971), 157, note 18; Pseudo-Callisthenes 1.22.4.

44. Ibid., 158, note 30; Plutarch, *De Cohibenda Ira* 8.

45. Plutach, *Moralia* 1.13d; as cited in Barth and Blanke, *Colossians*, 444, note 37.

46. See Dunn, *Colossians*, 258.

47. As cited in Scott Bartchy, "Slavery (Greco-Roman)," *ABD*, 6:69.

48. E. Beyreuther, "Like, Equal," *NIDNTT*, 2:499.

49. See Philo, *Good Person* 79.

50. See J. Jeremias, "θύρα," in *TDNT*, 3:174.

51. *Digesta* 48.3.8 (as cited in Brian Rapske, *The Book of Acts and Paul in Roman Custody* [BA1CS 3; Grand Rapids: Eerdmans, 1994], 27).

52. Timon as presented in Diogenes Laertius 4.67 (as cited in BAGD, 35).

53. See Eusebius, *History of the Church* 3.39.

54. W. Schneemelcher, ed., *New Testament Apocrypha* (Louisville, Ky.: Westminster/John Knox, 1992), 2.42–46.

Sidebar and Chart Notes

A-1. Plutarch, *Moralia* 164E–171F.

A-2. Plutarch, *Aemilius Paulus* 32–34.

A-3. Hippolytus, *Haer.* 9.11. Translation by J. H. MacMahon in *The Ante-Nicene Fathers*, vol. 5 (Grand Rapids: Eerdmans, n.d. [repr. 1990]).

A-4. For the Greek text and translation, see ibid., 64–66.

A-5. *Corpus Inscriptionum Judaicarum* 717.

A-6. *T. Sol.* 18:4, 7, 8, 15.

A-7. *Sepher Ha-Razim*, 4.25–30; cf. also 4.43–45. (The text is in: Michael Morgan, *Sepher Ha-Razim: The Book of Mysteries* [SBL Texts and Translations 25, Pseudepigrapha Series 11; Chico, Calif.: Scholars, 1983].)

A-8. Philo, *Spec. Laws* 2.233–36; trans. by F. H. Colson, *Philo* (LCL; Cambridge, Mass.: Harvard Univ. Press, 1984), with some modifications based on the Greek text.

PHILEMON

by S. M. Baugh

The Setting of Philemon

Philemon is the briefest of Paul's letters, consisting of only twenty-five verses. It is unlike Paul's other correspondence in that it is a private letter to an individual and to a house church. The closest equivalent is the letter to Titus, though even that has more general instructions for the benefit of others. There is no real objection to the genuineness of Pauline authorship, and the letter itself has been accepted as canonical from the earliest period, although it was not often cited in early Christian literature. The private nature of the subject matter makes the lack of citation of Philemon understandable.

A few scholars believe that Archippus (v. 2) was the addressee and owner of Onesimus, but this has not seemed likely to most. Philemon, by being addressed first in verse 1, is evidently the addressee and owner of Onesimus, and it was in his house that the church met (v. 2). An early tradition held that Apphia was the wife of Philemon and that Archippus was their son. This is a natural reading of verse 2,

COLOSSE

The unexcavated tel.

▶ Philemon
IMPORTANT FACTS:

- **AUTHOR:** The apostle Paul.
- **DATE:** About A.D. 60/61 (during Paul's first Roman imprisonment).
- **VENUES:** Paul is probably in prison in Rome writing to Philemon at Colosse.
- **OCCASION:**
  - To reconcile Philemon with his slave, Onesimus.
  - To tell of Paul's news to his fellow workers and to the church in Philemon's house.

but it cannot be substantiated beyond this. Because of connections between Philemon and the situation and people mentioned in Paul's letter to the Colossians, it is possible that Philemon was a resident of Colosse and that both Philemon and Colossians were written at roughly the same time. Because of this, commentaries on Philemon are often included with ones on the book of Colossians.[1]

The Occasion of Philemon

Paul was in prison when he wrote to Philemon (vv. 1 and 9); however, he hoped to be released and to stay with Philemon in the near future (see comments on v. 22). The occasion for this letter was the return of the slave Onesimus to his master; this is obvious enough in the letter. However, how the slave Onesimus of Colosse fell in with Paul in custody in Rome—halfway across the Mediterranean—is a problem. Some have proposed that Onesimus was sent to Paul by Philemon, then he somehow got into trouble with his master and needed restoring. But the letter seems more likely to suggest that Onesimus is a runaway slave. But if Onesimus were a runaway, why would he link up with Paul? It appears from verse 10 that Onesimus was not a

Christian when he first met Paul. But how could Onesimus come across Paul when he was in custody? Was Onesimus captured by the Roman authorities as a runaway? If that were the case, how could he, a prisoner, link up with Paul who was also in custody? All these issues have led most scholars to say that "somehow" Onesimus came into contact with Paul in Rome.

A recent suggestion, however, provides a compelling solution to the problem of Onesimus's contact with Paul.[2] Onesimus did not just run away from Philemon, but he ran away *to Paul* in order to secure Paul's aid in restoring him to his master's good graces for some reason. When a slave fell into his master's extreme disfavor, it could go very badly for him. In such cases, the slave had nothing but dismal prospects. In some cases they ran to one of their master's friends to beg his intercession (see comments below for examples). This scenario well explains how Onesimus could have met up with Paul: He sought him out. It also explains why Paul writes to secure Philemon's reconciliation with Onesimus and why Paul, not the Roman authorities, was sending Onesimus back to Philemon if he were a runaway. This will be the background assumed in my comments below.

Salutation and Letter Opening (1–3)

Paul does not open this letter with the usual identification of his apostolic office and summary of some aspects of the gospel. Instead, we have a brief identification of Paul as "a prisoner of Christ Jesus" (v. 1; cf. v. 9; i.e., a prisoner *for the sake of* Christ) and of "Timothy our brother," who was with Paul at this time. Next comes the identification of the recipients of the letter (v. 2) and a bene-

COLOSSE AND EPHESUS

Colosse was about 100 miles due east of Ephesus.
▼

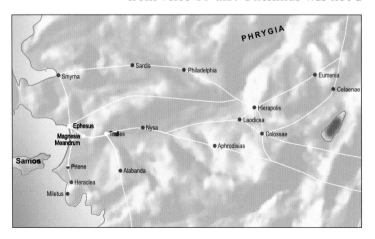

diction in the name of God the Father and of Jesus Christ (v. 3).

The letter is addressed to Philemon, "our dear friend and fellow worker" (v. 1; cf. v. 24 for other "fellow workers"). Paul and Philemon had developed a close association earlier, possibly while Paul was ministering in Ephesus (Acts 19). According to Colossians 4:9, Onesimus was from Colosse, so presumably his master Philemon was as well. Colosse lay about a hundred miles inland from Ephesus, connected by a route that went up the Maeander River valley and then passed through Laodicea to Colosse.

To Apphia our sister, to Archippus our fellow soldier (2). Early tradition and some today hold that Apphia was the wife of Philemon (known only from v. 2), which is possible but not certain. Some also believe that Archippus (Gk. "Commander of the horse") was the son of Philemon and Apphia, which is also possible. At the close of his instructions to the Colossian church, Paul writes: "Tell Archippus: 'See to it that you complete the work you have received in the Lord'" (Col. 4:17). It is possible that Archippus was ministering in Colosse and was for this reason Paul's "fellow soldier." If he were Philemon's son, it serves as further confirmation that this family and the church in their house were in Colosse.

And to the church that meets in your home (2). Paul also addresses the church meeting in Philemon's home (cf. Rom. 16:5; Col. 4:15). It is only natural that the church would need a place of meeting, and the home of a benefactor with its typical open inner courtyard would have supplied a suitable location.[3] Sometimes gatherings in these courtyards were made more pleasant through the erection of large and richly worked awnings covering the whole area—the sort of awnings that Paul himself may have dealt with in his capacity as a "tentmaker."[4]

Commendation of Philemon (4–7)

Your love has given me great joy and encouragement (7). Philemon has been active in sharing his faith by demonstrations of love for and service to his fellow Christians (vv. 5–7). Paul's praise for Philemon's service here is not forced flattery, but a sincere expression of his appreciation for the man's worthy service to Christ. This section of the letter shows that Paul is not domineering or demanding in his relations to Philemon, but truly considers him a friend worthy of his respect and admiration as a Christian brother who is also serving the Lord.

Intercession for Onesimus (8–22)

In Christ I could be bold and order you to do what you ought to do (8). To modern readers, this line may seem overbold, perhaps even threatening. However, to the ancient reader, this shows the complex interactions at work here. Paul may be "in chains" (v. 13) and Philemon may be his "dear friend" (v. 1)—perhaps even a wealthy and important friend—but Paul the apostle is his superior in the

SLAVE DOCUMENT

A first-century papyrus document recording the purchase of two slaves.

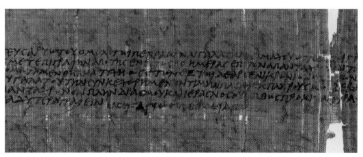

Lord. Paul does not bludgeon Philemon with this fact—one does not do that—but he does make it clear that what he is offering Philemon is the opportunity to obey him in this matter without losing face. Philemon's "obedience" (v. 21) to Paul can take the form of a spontaneous favor (v. 14), where he can "do even more than I ask" (v. 21).

Paul—an old man and now also a prisoner of Christ Jesus (9). As in verse 1, Paul says that he is "a prisoner of Christ Jesus." It was for the sake of Christ that he was "in chains for the gospel" (v. 13; cf. v. 23). Similarly, the early second-century Christian bishop Ignatius of Antioch went to Rome for his martyrdom "in bondage in Christ Jesus," chained between a rough troop of soldiers.[5] Paul's Roman imprisonment was a rough, frustrating period for him, though not entirely unfruitful for the gospel since Onesimus "became my son while I was in chains" (v. 10; cf. Acts 28). Paul made converts to Christ even in custody awaiting his trial.[6]

▶ Patronage in the Roman World

The letters of the younger Pliny are particularly helpful in showing patronage at work in the Roman world. Every day, a Roman noble would attend to the morning visit of his "clients," in whose troubles and concerns he would intercede. If a man wished to find a husband for his daughter, his patron would recommend and arrange a suitable match.[A-1] He might also supply the girl with a proper dowry.[A-2] If a man wished to rise in station and enter the rank (*ordo*) of the "knights" (*equites*), his patron would supply the requisite funds.[A-3] A patron would intercede in land purchase.[A-4] A highly placed patron could even ask for grant of civil, religious, or military offices for his "friends" or other benefits, such as grant of citizenship for his clients, which included his freedmen.[A-5] This system was a code of honor and debt under the name of "friendship" (Latin, *amicitia*): "For, according to the code of friendship, the one who takes the initiative puts the other in his debt and owes no more until he is repaid."[A-6] A patron was not optional in such a world: "No one can make a start, however outstanding his abilities, if he lacks scope and opportunity *and a patron to support him.*"[A-7] And patronage was not confined to the interaction of individuals. Whole towns and villages were under the patronage of certain nobles, whose citizens could count on favors and assistance provided they showed the proper honors to their "godfather."[A-8]

Paul's subtle maneuvers with Philemon in verses 8–22 are only understood against the background of the ancient patronage system, which worked on many different levels of Greco-Roman society (see comments in the accompanying box).[A-9] As the owner and head of his household, Philemon was in every way the patron of Onesimus. For Paul to meddle in this family relationship—for slaves were members of the family—took utmost delicacy and a twofold claim. (1) Paul must either be Philemon's superior and patron or, if they were roughly equals, Philemon must owe him a debt of friendship, which Paul could claim as needing repayment in the matter at hand. This is the reason why Paul subtly suggests that Philemon owes him, as it were, even his very self (v. 19). Eternal life is a debt of great importance indeed! (2) Paul must establish that he has some claim of patronage on the slave Onesimus. It was the duty of a patron to pay the debts of members of his household, yet Paul intercedes for Onesimus directly, when he says: "If he has done you any wrong or owes you anything, charge it to me.... I will pay it back" (vv. 18–19). This is unmistakably the act of a patron, and it makes Paul's intercession for Onesimus all the more effective; yet would not have given offense to Philemon, who perfectly understood and accepted Paul's points.

▶ Manumission and Paul

Ancient slavery strikes the modern reader as a cruel institution. Indeed, it sometimes could be very cruel. Why then did not Paul speak out against it, or why did he not simply order Philemon to manumit Onesimus instead of sending him back? The answer involves knowing first that manumission of a slave often did not change his situation much. He simply became a freedman, though he might still remain in the same situation within his former master's household—only his legal status having changed. The Greco-Roman world was very much *family-oriented*, and for a slave to be manumitted and sent out of the household would actually be potentially greatly disadvantageous. Without a family, he would have no immediate social, legal, or occupational connections. Nevertheless, F. F. Bruce was correct to say that the letter to Philemon "brings us into an atmosphere in which the institution [of slavery] could only wilt and die."[A-10] And in the letter of Philemon, Paul applied what he preached: in Christ there is neither slave nor free (Gal. 3:28).

My son Onesimus (10). "Onesimus" means "profitable or "beneficial" in Greek and is a common slave name. Paul comes close to punning on this name in verse 11, saying that though Onesimus was formerly "useless" to Philemon, now he was "useful" (Gk. *euchrēston*).[7] Paul does carry on the pun, however, when he says that he wishes Philemon to accede to his wishes, in order that "I may have some *benefit* from you" (v. 20; emphasis added). The Greek verb form for "to have benefit" used in verse 20 is etymologically related to the name "Onesimus."

Paul mentioned Onesimus in Colossians 4:9 as "our faithful and dear brother, who is one of you"; thus we assume that Onesimus—and therefore Philemon—lived in Colosse. Where Onesimus came from originally is impossible to tell. He could have been a "house-born" slave, born to one of Philemon's slaves and therefore an indentured member of the household. Or he could have been purchased from outside the household, a foundling infant raised into slavery perhaps.[8]

As I noted in the introduction, it seems most likely that Onesimus intentionally ran away from Philemon and ran *to* Paul in order to seek his intercession on his behalf with Philemon over some quarrel between the master and slave. This letter is Paul's intercession. We know of other such cases (see accompanying box for one). A master vexed with a slave might put him to death in extreme cases (though this meant a significant loss of property, for a slave was regarded as property).[9] More commonly, the slave would be beaten, demoted to menial jobs, or sent away to hard labor on the family farm, in a mill, or in some other brutally arduous occupation. Faced with such a prospect, Onesimus, who undoubtedly knew of Philemon's high regard for Paul, fled to him and found him in Rome. But in the course of events, Onesimus became a Christian (v. 10), and therefore Paul was sending Onesimus back to Philemon (v. 12) as his brother in Christ (v. 16) as well as a beloved helper to Paul, who served in Philemon's absence at his side (vv. 12–13, 16).

I, Paul, am writing this with my own hand (19). Paul adds a concluding note in his own hand in other letters.[10] Paul probably dictated his letters, but perhaps he subscribed his own greetings as an authentication of the letter. Philemon, on the other hand, was probably wholly written by Paul.[11]

Prepare a guest room for me (22). The way Paul asks Philemon to "prepare" a room for him (v. 22) means something more like, "hold a room in readiness for me." Paul did not know when he would be released, and he asks Philemon to be prepared for some distant eventuality.

Closing and Greetings (23–25)

Paul closes his letter with the greetings of his companions: Epaphras, Mark, Aristarchus, Demas, and Luke. These men were his "fellow workers," as was Philemon himself (v. 1). The letter concludes with an apostolic blessing in the name of the Lord Jesus Christ.

▶ Intercession for a Slave

Cassius Dio provides an instructive description of a man's intercession with his friend on behalf of a slave. The intercessor is the Emperor Augustus and the slave owner is the famously cruel Vedius Pollio, who kept a pool filled with man-eating eels into which he would throw errant slaves. Dio describes the incident like this:

Once, when he [Vedius Pollio] was entertaining Augustus, his cup-bearer broke a crystal goblet. Thereupon Pollio, paying no attention to his guest, ordered the slave to be thrown to the eels. The boy fell on his knees before Augustus and implored his protection, and the emperor at first tried to persuade Pollio not to commit so appalling an action. When Pollio paid no heed, Augustus said, "Bring all your other drinking vessels like this one, or any others of value that you possess for me to use." When these were brought, he ordered them to be smashed. Pollio was naturally vexed at the sight; but since he could no longer be angry about the one goblet in view of the multitude of others that had been destroyed, and could not punish his servant for an act which Augustus had repeated, he restrained himself and said nothing.[A-11]

ANNOTATED BIBLIOGRAPHY

Bruce, F. F. *The Epistles to the Colossians, to Philemon, and to the Ephesians.* NICNT. Grand Rapids: Eerdmans, 1984.

> Bruce had a wide knowledge of the ancient world and applies it in all his commentaries with great benefit and soundness.

Lightfoot, J. B. *Saint Paul's Epistles to the Colossians and to Philemon.* London and New York: Macmillan, 1890.

> Even though it is dated, Lightfoot's commentary is still profitable, full of rich insights into the ancient world and into biblical and early patristic texts.

O'Brien, Peter T. *Colossians, Philemon.* WBC. Waco: Word, 1982.

> O'Brien's works are always scholarly and reliable. His comments on Philemon are no exception.

Wright, N. T. *The Epistles of Paul to the Colossians and to Philemon.* TNTC. Grand Rapids: Eerdmans, 1986.

> This commentary series always provides useful material. Wright's comments are brief but helpful.

Main Text Notes

1. For general introduction see D. A. Carson, Douglas J. Moo and Leon Morris, *An Introduction to the New Testament* (Grand Rapids: Zondervan, 1992), 387–90.

2. The original suggestion is that of Peter Lampe, "Keine 'Sklavenflucht' des Onesimus," *ZNW* 76 (1985): 135–37; summarized and expanded in B. M. Rapske, "The Prisoner Paul in the Eyes of Onesimus," *NTS* 37 (1991): 187–203 and S. Scott Bartchy, "Philemon, Epistle To," *ABD*, 5:305–9; cf. *New Docs* 8 (1998): 1–46.

3. Cf. Robert J. Banks, *Paul's Idea of Community: The Early House Churches in Their Cultural Setting* (Peabody, Mass.: Hendrikson, 1994); Bradley Blue, "Acts and the House Church," in *The Book of Acts in Its Graeco-Roman Setting* (D. W. J. Gill and C. Gempf, eds.; Grand Rapids and Carlisle: Eerdmans and Paternoster, 1994), 119–222.

4. See Peter Lampe, "Paulus—Zeltmacher," *BZ* 31 (1987): 256–61; Steven M. Baugh, "Paul and Ephesus: The Apostle Among His Contemporaries" (Ph.D. diss.; Irvine, Calif.: Univ. of California, 1990), 101–19.

5. Ignatius, *Romans* 1.1. 5.1; cf. *Philadelphians* 5.1–2.

6. See the full treatment of Brian Rapske, *The Book of Acts and Paul in Roman Custody* (Grand Rapids and Carlisle: Eerdmans and Paternoster, 1994); cf. Harry W. Tajra, *The Trial of St. Paul* (WUNT 35; Tübingen: J. C. B. Mohr, 1989).

7. Cf. Plato, *Republic* 411A; Shepherd of Hermas, *Vision* 3.6.7; *Mandata* 5.6.6 for other contrasts between useful and useless.

8. "Foundlings" were infants rejected by their parents at birth and left somewhere to die, who were then picked up and raised by someone else. Often foundlings became the slaves of their finders, who might make a business of finding and raising children into slavery (as we know from extant papyrus nursing contracts from Egypt). For a handy collection of documents see Thomas Wiedemann, *Greek and Roman Slavery* (Baltimore and London: Johns Hopkins Univ. Press, 1981).

9. Cf. Martin Hengel, *Crucifixion* (Philadelphia: Fortress, 1977), 51–63 for crucifixion as *servile supplicium*, "the slaves' punishment."

10. 1 Cor. 16:21; Gal. 6:11; Col. 4:18.

11. Cf. E. R. Richards, *The Secretary in the Letters of Paul* (WUNT 2/42; Tübingen: J. C. B. Mohr [Paul Siebeck], 1991).

Sidebar and Chart Notes

A-1. Pliny, *Ep.* 1.13.

A-2. Ibid., 2.4; 6.32.

A-3. Ibid., 1.19.

A-4. Ibid., 1.24.

A-5. Ibid., 2.9, 13; 3.2, 8; 4.4, 17; 6.25; 10.12; cf. 10.13; 10.6–7, 10–11.

A-6. Ibid., 7.31.

A-7. Cf. A. N. Sherwin-White, *The Letters of Pliny: A Historical and Social Commentary* (Oxford: Clarendon, 1966), ad loc; Pliny, *Ep.* 6.23 (emphasis added).

A-8. E.g., Pliny, *Ep.* 3.4; 4.1.

A-9. Cf. Richard P. Saller, *Personal Patronage under the Early Empire* (Cambridge: Cambridge Univ. Press, 1982).

A-10. F. F. Bruce, *Paul: Apostle of the Heart Set Free* (Exeter and Grand Rapids: Paternoster and Eerdmans, 1977), 401.

A-11. Cassius Dio, *Roman History* 54.23, Penguin trans.

CREDITS FOR PHOTOS AND MAPS

Arnold, Clinton E. . . . . pp. 8, 21(2), 27, 40, 72–73, 75, 76, 83, 85, 101, 106–7
Bredow, Dennis . . . . pp. 6, 46
Dunn, Cheryl (for Talbot Bible Lands) . . . . pp. 48, 50
Haradine, Jane (public domain photos) . . . . p. 81
Isachar, Hanan . . . . p. 20
King, Jay . . . . p. 39(2)
Kohlenberger, John R. III . . . . pp. 4(2), 47, 48, 74, 108
Konstas, Ioannis . . . . pp. 93, 112
Radovan, Zev . . . . pp. 10, 18, 34, 50, 53
Rigsby, Richard . . . . p. 33
Ritmeyer, Leen . . . . p. 21
University of Michigan . . . . pp. 13, 38, 52, 65, 90, 92, 109
Zondervan Image Archive (Neal Bierling) . . . . pp. 2–3, 5(2), 14, 15, 17, 23, 30, 32, 49, 55, 59, 60

ALSO AVAILABLE

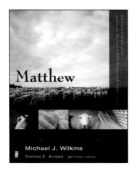

Matthew

Michael J. Wilkins
Clinton E. Arnold general editor

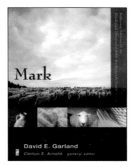

Mark

David E. Garland
Clinton E. Arnold general editor

Luke

Mark L. Strauss
Clinton E. Arnold general editor

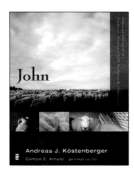

John

Andreas J. Köstenberger
Clinton E. Arnold general editor

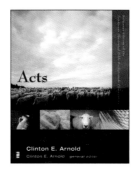

Acts

Clinton E. Arnold
Clinton E. Arnold general editor

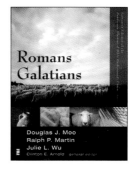

Romans
Galatians

Douglas J. Moo
Ralph P. Martin
Julie L. Wu
Clinton E. Arnold general editor

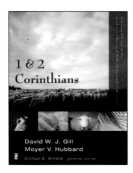

1 & 2
Corinthians

David W. J. Gill
Moyer V. Hubbard
Clinton E. Arnold general editor

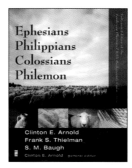

Ephesians
Philippians
Colossians
Philemon

Clinton E. Arnold
Frank S. Thielman
S. M. Baugh
Clinton E. Arnold general editor

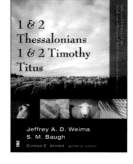

1 & 2
Thessalonians
1 & 2 Timothy
Titus

Jeffrey A. D. Weima
S. M. Baugh
Clinton E. Arnold general editor

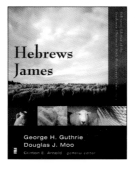

Hebrews
James

George H. Guthrie
Douglas J. Moo
Clinton E. Arnold general editor

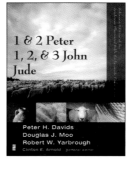

1 & 2 Peter
1, 2, & 3 John
Jude

Peter H. Davids
Douglas J. Moo
Robert W. Yarbrough
Clinton E. Arnold general editor

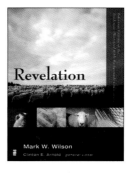

Revelation

Mark W. Wilson
Clinton E. Arnold general editor